UTPAL DUTT

Born in 1929 in Barishal (now in Bangladesh), Utpal Dutt began his theatrical career in college at St Xavier's, Calcutta, playing in selected scenes from *Romeo and Juliet*, *Macbeth* and *Richard III*. In 1947, he found his 'guru'—Geoffrey Kendal, and his life with the strolling Kendals lasted 'from August 1947 to the end of 1948, and again from February 1953 to the end of 1954'. Dutt's first significant directorial experiment was a modern-dress version of *Julius Caesar* in 1949, for the group Amateur Shakespeareans. This group was later renamed Little Theatre Group in 1950, and moved to productions in Bengali. Real popular success came with *Angar* in 1959 at Minerva (taken on a 'long lease' in 1959), followed by *Ferari Fouj*, *Titash* and *Kallol*. *Kallol* made a savage criticism of the Congress, the party in power in 1965, and D̶ ⸻ ᵕ̶as immediately arrested and detained in Presidency Jail without ⸻ March 1966, he did a series of documentary plays at ⸻ movement, going underground in 196⸻ when he turned up for the shooting of ⸻ on the intervention of his American pro⸻ he took up his first assignment in the Jatra and went on to write ⸻ *Rifle*. Between 1968 and 1972, he wrote and directed 17 Jatra plays. Wanting to explore the form further, he formed the Vivek Jatra Samaj (for rural and suburban audiences) and People's Little Theatre for the urban proscenium. PLT survived and it was the immediate success of its *Tiner Talwar* in 1971 that ensured a second run for Dutt. PLT went on to deliver more hits, including *Barricade* (1972) and *Dushwapner Nagari* (1974).

Dutt was also acquiring a reputation as a film actor, both in Calcutta and in Bombay. Major performances include either lead or supporting roles in films like Satyajit Ray's *Jana Aranya* (The Middleman) and *Agantuk* (The Stranger); Mrinal Sen's *Bhuvan Shome* and *Chorus*; and James Ivory's *Shakespearewallah* and *The Guru*.

A prolific writer, he has left behind a vast quantity of writings on theatre, literature and cinema as well as the monographs *Towards A Revolutionary Theatre*, *Shakespeare-er Samaj Chetona* and *Girish Manash*.

Recipient of the National Award for Best Actor in *Bhuvan Shome* in 1970 and a Fellow of the Sangeet Natak Akademi (1990), Dutt died in 1993.

BARRICADE

Utpal Dutt

TRANSLATED FROM THE TEXT AND THE PRODUCTION
BY ANANDA LAL

LONDON NEW YORK CALCUTTA

Seagull Books 2021

Introduction and English translation © Ananda Lal, 2021

Original Bengali text, and performance rights © Bishnupriya Dutt

ISBN 978 1 8030 9 051 1

British Library Cataloguing-in-Publication Data
A catalogue record for this book is available from the British Library

Typeset by Seagull Books, Calcutta, India
Printed and bound in New Delhi by WordsWorth India

To the memory of
Professors Burnet M. Hobgood (1922–2000)
and Robert B. Graves (1946–2020),
my gurus at the Department of Theatre, University of Illinois,
who first encouraged me to translate drama
and gave me the confidence to believe in my stylistic method

CONTENTS

INTRODUCTION
Ananda Lal

Historians of Bengali theatre agree that, among playwrights in the second half of the twentieth century, Badal Sircar (1925–2011) and Utpal Dutt (1929–93) stand the tallest in view of their sustained and qualitative contribution to original drama, of over fifty plays each. Several of Sircar's scripts have been translated into English, starting in 1971 with *There's No End*, published in *Enact* magazine, and then 1974 with his landmark *Evam Indrajit* (in one of those oddities of past translation practice, rendered in English by Girish Karnad, who did not know Bengali). However, strangely enough, Dutt's plays never received the same recognition, even though his first English translation, *Invincible Vietnam*, had appeared much earlier, in 1967. As a result, non-Bengalis have not had direct access to the range and wealth of his oeuvre, in spite of the fact that he is acknowledged nationally as among the trailblazers of post-Independence theatre in India.

To summarize for our purposes here Dutt's accomplishments, I turn to the leading Bengali critic Kironmoy Raha, a most elegant writer in English (who, coincidentally, translated Sircar's above-mentioned *There's No End*):

> a staunch Marxist [. . . h]e joined the Indian People's Theatre Association but left after a couple of years [. . .] he soon established himself as the foremost proponent of political theatre with a pronounced leftist orientation.

[. . .] Dutt staged his *Angar* ('Coal', 1959) on a coal-mine disaster, the first of a series of spectacular productions in which he aimed to cast a spell on audiences through the use of lights, sound, music, visual grandeur, tense acting, and melodramatic situations. He eminently succeeded: the spell held viewers captive and receptive to the message. [. . .]

[. . .] Dutt's demoniac energy and indomitable determination [. . .] put up powerful plays like *Tiner taloyar* ('Tin Sword', 1971) and *Duhswapner nagari* ('Nightmare City', 1974). [. . .] They bore the stamp of his dazzling talent, prolific output, comic acting, unerring sense of theatricality, grasp over stagecraft, and orchestration of diverse elements with a conductor's assurance.

[. . . He] wrote serious studies of Shakespeare, Girish Ghosh, Stanislavsky, Brecht, and revolutionary theatre, and translated Shakespeare and Brecht. A measure of his prodigious industry and productivity is that he authored twenty-two full-length plays, fifteen poster plays, nineteen Jatra scripts, acted in thousands of shows, and directed more than sixty productions. Few in Bengali theatre history matched his many-sided personality and achievements.[1]

---

1 Kironmoy Raha, 'Dutt, Utpal', in Ananda Lal (ed.), *The Oxford Companion to Indian Theatre* (New Delhi: Oxford University Press, 2004), pp. 115–16. Depending on how one defines 'full-length', the count of 22 can increase to around 30 original plays directed by Dutt himself, excluding adaptations and a few staged by other groups. 'Poster plays' is the term Dutt used for street-corner theatre, and Jatra is the most popular traditional Bengali folk form. Several Dutt plays had double incarnations under different titles for the proscenium and Jatra respectively; Raha seems to have categorized them according to the genre in which they were first performed.

Raha did not mention *Barricade* (1972) in this entry, but had found it 'stunning' and even better than *Tiner taloyār* in his review of the original production when it travelled to New Delhi in early 1973.[2] Rustom Bharucha, present at its opening night in Calcutta but writing in 1982, attested to its place and impact in Dutt's work and also used the word 'stunned':

> *Barricade* is unanimously considered the most staggering spectacle in the contemporary Bengali theater. A huge shadow of Hitler gesticulating like a madman, intricately choreographed street fights, a balletic Red Flag sequence, meticulously timed bursts of deafening music, constructivist scenery with stark outlines, the jury sitting with their backs to the audience in the orchestra pit—these are some of *Barricade*'s memorable theatrical effects.
>
> One is simply stunned by the production's momentum.[3]

The immediate trigger for *Barricade* was both political and topical. West Bengal, under President's Rule as the ultra-left Naxalite movement began to crumble in 1971, was passing through extreme instability (coupled with bearing the brunt of the refugee influx from East Pakistan during Bangladesh's liberation struggle). Hemanta Basu, the respected 75-year-old leader of the leftist

---

2 Kironmoy Raha, 'Utpal Dutt's Barricade Memorable'. Name of newspaper not recorded in the clipping held by Natya Shodh Sansthan, Kolkata, dated by hand as February 1973. *Barricade* had three performances in Delhi, on 11, 14 and 16 February.

3 Rustom Bharucha, *Rehearsals of Revolution: The Political Theater of Bengal* (Calcutta: Seagull Books, 1983), pp. 106–07. The play premiered at Kala Mandir, a modern 1000-seater auditorium with an orchestra pit. Dutt himself termed the set Constructivist in the manner of Tairov: '*People's Little Theatre-r sādhāran bārshik sabhāy pathita parichālaker report*', *Epic Theatre* (November–February–May 1973): *v*.

Forward Bloc party, had been stabbed to death in February 1971 as he was about to board a taxi outside Calcutta, which had seen many politically-motivated assassinations of late. Occurring just before general elections in March, the killing horrified citizenry, who spontaneously joined the funeral procession. The Congress Party and others blamed the Communist Party of India (Marxist) for the murder, placing it on their campaign plank for the legislative assembly elections in Bengal, held simultaneously. Nevertheless, as pointed out astutely by Dutt, 'the CPI (M) emerged as the largest single party in the state'.[4] However, a coalition led by the Congress formed the government, lasting merely three months before collapsing into another spell of President's Rule.

In 1972, West Bengal went to the polls again. Dutt recalled those days in an interview:

> There was no way we could do political plays in Calcutta at that point of time, with the Congress mafia on the rampage. They were killing people. CPI (M) offices were being attacked everywhere, set on fire. Party workers were being dragged out of their homes and being killed.
>
> [. . .] But in 1972 we all felt that we had to take the offensive. Then we staged *Barricade*. They were making a Reichstag Fire trial out of the murder of Hemanta Basu. They were trying to put the guilt on the communists and hoping to win the elections that way.[5]

---

4 Utpal Dutt, *Towards a Revolutionary Theatre* (Calcutta: M. C. Sarkar & Sons, 1982), p. 91.

5 'Utpal Dutt: An Interview by Samik Bandyopadhyay', in *Contemporary Indian Theatre*: *Interviews with Playwrights and Directors* (New Delhi: Sangeet Natak Akademi, 1989), pp. 17–18.

In his words, 'shameless rigging [. . .] they carried out in 1972 elections, shooting and bombing voters away, capturing booths, stuffing ballot-paper into the box at the point of sten-guns [. . .] and to the shame of the intellectuals, not one voice was raised against this naked aggression against democracy.' And the Congress came to power. Thus, 'out of sheer anger' he conceived *Barricade*.[6]

Dutt found near-identical parallels to the situation in 1933 Germany, a period he had visited earlier when he translated into Bengali the internationally-successful *Professor Mamlock* by the German dramatist Friedrich Wolf (1888–1953) in 1964. He based *Barricade* loosely on the Nazi takeover in 1933 as outlined in the fictionalized chronicle *Unsere Strasse* by Jan Petersen (1906–69), translated into English as *Our Street*, and depicting the brave Communist resistance at Wallstrasse in Berlin. Dutt had consulted both the German and English texts (his wife, Sova Sen, had given me his copy of the German book to help in my subtitling of the video recording), but the play remains his own original creation, most of the characters having little in common with Petersen's, and the others entirely from Dutt's imagination. In addition, he acknowledged the following sources:

William Shirer's *The Rise and Fall of the Third Reich* (for German election history) and *Berlin Diary*

Hermann Rauschning's *Hitler Speaks* (for Hitler's two speeches)

Alan Bullock's *Hitler: A Study in Tyranny*

Hugh Trevor-Roper's *The Last Days of Hitler*

Hitler's *Mein Kampf*

---

6 Dutt, *Revolutionary Theatre*, pp. 91–2.

Roger Manvell and Heinrich Fraenkel's *Doctor Goebbels* and *Goering*[7]

The decision to ostensibly dramatize history and describe *Barricade* as a 'historical drama'[8] was a wise move that protected him from political vendetta and prosecution, whereas spectators understood the implications without any difficulty. Raha vouched as much: 'the play [. . .] reflects a situation very similar to one in West Bengal before the mid-term elections.'[9] As witnessed by Bharucha, 'I can still hear the audience cheer the climactic moments of the trial and abuse the Congress government with gusto.'[10] Dutt himself commented about the reactions:

> We were glad we had given theatrical expression to our wrath and the people, deprived of all rights, seemed to see their own fury bursting in the lines of the text. But of course the IPTA [Indian People's Theatre Association] and the windbags in its leadership found nothing in the play worth liking, and though they themselves were doing absolutely nothing, so scared were they of the Congress brownshirts, they furiously attacked our play, and thereby strengthened the morale of the brownshirts. The rightist CPI [Communist Party of India] also attacked 'Barricade' through their organ.[11]

---

7 Dutt credited these books in some playbills distributed at various performances, but not in the printed editions.

8 In the very first sentence of the note on the play in the playbills mentioned above.

9 Raha, 'Utpal Dutt's Barricade Memorable'.

10 Bharucha, *Rehearsals of Revolution*, p. 108.

11 Dutt, *Revolutionary Theatre*, p. 92.

Readers today may feel surprised to learn that several Bengali critics wrote lengthy, scathing vilifications of *Barricade* as not Communistic enough—in other words, for not showing the German Communist resistance as wholly idealistic or heroic (let alone victorious), and for depicting them as a ragtag bag of uncommitted individuals, some of them given to drinking and mouthing obscenities. No doubt the purist doctrines of Soviet socialist realism ignited these broadsides. The Marxist theatre monthly *Abhinay* called Dutt a 'babu intellectual' and concluded with the jibe that he should follow the final exhortation of his own Sutradhar in the Prologue: 'think of your own story, worry about your own homeland. You don't have to worry about the German population in 1933.'[12] An article in the theatre quarterly *Nātya Prasanga* labelled the play with the Bengali equivalents of 'revisionist' and 'counter-revolutionary', favourite leftist insults of those times, for overlooking the dedication of India's working-class rebels.[13] Dutt in turn roundly denigrated these 'moronic'[14] critics as ignorant, singling out the reviewer in the leading Communist magazine *Frontier*, edited by Dutt's friend, the famous poet Samar Sen.

Later performances of *Barricade* did not go unopposed. Sova Sen recorded in her diary that the Communist Party of India

12 'Bhrānta buddhir gananātya—ganikābrittir Barricade', *Abhinay* (September–October 1972): 1647–50. The date may confuse readers, for *Barricade* premiered in December. But Soumitra Kumar Chatterjee, the authority on *Abhinay*, confirmed to me that its publication schedule had been upset, as happened regularly in Bengal during the turmoil following the Naxal unrest, and this issue appeared later.

13 Sudrak, 'Utpal Datter Barricade biplaber madhye pratibitlah', *Nātya Prasanga* (September 1973): 70–95.

14 The word he used several times in 'People's Little Theatre-r sādhāran bārshik sabhāy pathita parichālaker report' is *murkha*.

revoked an invitation in 1973.[15] Dutt described the curious circumstances as follows:

> the CPI, true to its politics of subservience to the Indira
> [Gandhi, Prime Minister of India] dictatorship, created a
> particularly revolting scandal with regard to 'Barricade'.
> They were about to hold a youth festival in Calcutta, and
> [. . .] two of their leaders paid me a sudden visit. One of
> them, Comrade Moni Sanyal, was a much-respected
> friend of mine. They insisted that the PLT [People's Little
> Theatre, Dutt's group] join the festival with 'Barricade'. I
> said, 'We shall certainly be glad to join the youth festival,
> but I suggest some other play, such as The Tin Sword
> [*Tiner taloyār*]. As the first convenor, I know the youth fes-
> tival platform should not be used for political theatre'. But
> Comrade Sanyal insisted on 'Barricade', because he said
> it would fill the stadium.
>
> On the morning of the performance after our sets
> had arrived in the stadium, Comrade Sanyal and Mr.
> Gurudas Dasgupta came post-haste to my house, to beg
> us not to play 'Barricade', but 'The Tin Sword'. I said,
> 'What has happened?' 'Pressure', they said, 'endless pres-
> sure.' I said, 'Any change of programme is now out of the
> question. I had warned you about this. Now it's too late.
> Either we play Barricade or we don't play at all.'
>
> We were not allowed to play at all. [. . .] Thus the
> first attempt to censor plays under Indira Gandhi's rule
> came, not from the Congress, but from the rightist com-
> munists. Thereafter, Barricade ran into rough waters.

---

15 Sova Sen, *Smarane Bismarane* (Kolkata: M. C. Sarkar & Sons, 1993),
p. 115.

Gangs of heavily-armed and drink-crazed rogues would regularly visit us backstage and warn us not to say anything against the Lady. We would counter it with a simple argument: The play is about Hitler, why does that hurt you? Do you then admit that the cap fits, that you are Nazis? They usually left after that.[16]

Barricade refers to the Nazis attacking a theatre in Berlin. Shockingly, in 1974 the same kind of violence came to pass in the experience of Dutt's group when Congress goondas ransacked the Star Theatre and assaulted the cast and crew preparing for a show of his *Duhswapner Nagari*.[17] Dutt recounts:

I saw Tapas Sen, India's foremost expert of lighting, being knocked down by a bunch of thugs. Sabita Banerjee, actress, was dragged by her hair down the road. [. . .]

[. . .] I must record here the courage of the local residents who formed a knot around my wife, Sova Sen, and protected her from the mob.[18]

The following year, Indira Gandhi succeeded in having Emergency declared.

One must demolish the critical cliche that Dutt's partisan faith dictated him to write propagandist drama, and therefore he constructed cardboard characters. The six main individuals in *Barricade* certainly do not conform to this misconception, while representing important functions of democracy: the media, the

---

16 Dutt, *Revolutionary Theatre*, pp. 92–3.

17 See Utpal Dutt, *Three Plays* (Calcutta: Seagull Books, 2009), which includes *Duhswapner Nagari* translated as *Nightmare City*.

18 Dutt, *Revolutionary Theatre*, p. 93. Tapas Sen, Sabita Bandyopadhyay (Banerjee) and Sova Sen were also in the team of *Barricade*.

polity, the judiciary, the intelligentsia, the citizenry. The protagonist Otto, an investigative journalist who remains doggedly independent, practises a professional dedication to fact-checking and truth, and ultimately places ethics over domestic safety-first concerns. Even the antagonist, SS leader Lippert, surprisingly declares in court that witch-hunting is anti-people: 'We shouldn't pay heed to this sort of leaflet unless we're absolutely certain. Because then it won't be a killer's trial any longer, it'll get transformed into a comprehensive blow against an entire political group. That'll be the grave of German democracy.' We might be tempted to take him at face value and approve of his sentiment, locating him among the liberal factions of the Nazis in 1933. More likely, he deliberately speaks disingenuously here, like the Nazi Party had done initially. This recurrent streak of irony in Dutt's writing rises immediately when Otto's boss, the co-opted owner-editor Landt, reacts appreciatively about Lippert's seeming fairness, 'People say about these Nazis, they're enemies of democracy!' With politicians and press complicit, Dutt reposes the greatest trust in the legal system, in the person of the impartial Justice Voss who virtually threatens Lippert with contempt of court in his last appearance—just before the Nazis do away with him.

Dutt wants intellectuals and commoners to stand up as strong as Voss, not become compromised. He reprises the character of the uncommitted Dr Mamlock in *Barricade* as Dr Strubbel, who distances himself from current affairs and prefers reading literature instead. But in the end, after the Nazis infamously set books ablaze in front of Humboldt University, Strubbel's conscience stirs: 'If I have to survive by carrying out their commands, where's my respect for reading Schopenhauer and Karl Marx? They're burning books, understand?' Yet even in tragedy, Dutt never loses his ironic sense of humour, when Strubbel sits down at the barricade and jumps up instantly with the exclamation, 'Oof, what dust.

Suppose, during the lulls in the war I can recite Goethe's poems to you. That will increase your morale.' The privileged cannot forget their dust-phobia and verse-philia.

Dutt's portrait of the widow Ingeborg Zauritz, whose assassinated husband is his fictive equivalent of Hemanta Basu, is the most complex. She rejects violent extremism categorically and is a devout Catholic: 'I'm not a Communist, I don't know anything except Jesus.' When the Nazis capture and torture their adopted son Paul, she says 'You're the end of civilization. You're crucifying Jesus again.' In a dream sequence after the Nazis shoot Paul in cold blood, she sees him (in the stage direction) *standing like Jesus in a white robe and with a crown of thorns on his head.*' A Christian-Communist martyr, a contradiction in terms, Paul quotes from the Bible: 'I haven't come to distribute peace. I've come to create rifts between father and son, brother and brother. I've come to give the sword.' Inge repeats these lines on the barricade as her motto in the finale, before which she verbalizes her realization, 'Now I understand, the Communists die first, then the others' turns come one by one, then—then one day I see the entire country's a jail-house.'

Just as he resolves apparent ideological contradictions, Dutt masterfully unites traditional Indian and Brechtian dramaturgies. He sets the Prologue to *Barricade* in the here and now, in contemporary Kolkata, before transporting us for the play proper to the there and then. The convention of the Sutradhar introducing his drama and its dramatis personae links popular Bengali forms like the Jatra with other Indian folk theatres as well as the elitist Sanskrit classics like *Sakuntalā* (which, significantly, describes the callousness of royal rulers; Dutt never disowned classical masterpieces outright). But the closer political connection lies with Brecht, whose *Caucasian Chalk Circle* uses the identical structure— a Prologue in modern-day USSR that introduces the parable from ancient times—and, like *Barricade*, does not have to return to the present at the conclusion, except for a song (explicatory in Brecht, rousing in Dutt), because the parable has made its point. However, I should qualify that Dutt insisted *Barricade* had nothing to do with Brechtian form as it was intended for 'our' spectators, who liked highly 'impassioned' drama.[19]

Rustom Bharucha commented nearly forty years ago, '*Barricade* demonstrates that a political allegory is essentially time bound. It loses much of its significance when it is revived. Its specificity of detail is at once its strength and limitation.'[20] On the contrary, I believe that history repeats itself, as it did in 1971-72, recalling events of four decades before in Germany. Consequently, the purpose of political theatre through the prismatic means of Brechtian alienation-effect, alluding to the past as a warning to the present, retains utmost validity. Today, the surge to power of far-right parties and fundamentalist fanaticism across the world means that the co-option of democracy and civil society in 1933 leading to Nazi fascism can happen again—or indeed has already happened—restoring to a work like *Barricade* its immediate urgency.

Texts

Barricade first appeared in book form on 1 May 1977, published by Jatiya Sahitya Parishad in Kolkata. It was included in the fifth volume of Dutt's complete plays, *Nātak Samagra*, published by Mitra & Ghosh, Kolkata, in 1997. The two texts are substantially the same, except for minor corrections carried out in the later edition. However, some inadvertent errors also crept into this

---

19 Dutt, '*People's Little Theatre-r sādhāran bārshik sabhāy pathita parichālaker report*', p. *iii*.

20 Bharucha, *Rehearsals of Revolution*, p. 108.

definitive edition. Therefore, I consulted both and, where the occasional discrepancies arose, adopted readings from the first edition if I thought they reflected Dutt's intentions better. My foot-notes to those instances explain my rationale.

Until very recently, researchers of Indian theatre did not have access to video recordings of productions, the technology for which became more affordable to groups only in the 1990s. I consider myself extremely fortunate to have been associated with the 1995 telecast of *Barricade* by the Central Production Centre of Doordarshan, India's state television network. The director, Abhijit Dasgupta, producer at Doordarshan, had asked me to sub-title it in English for the benefit of their national audience. I pre-served the VHS tape copy in my possession, fully aware of its archival value. It served as the third text for my translation, not only confirming that the People's Little Theatre production fol-lowed Dutt's printed text virtually verbatim, but also clarifying some curious issues in the script and throwing considerable light on stage business that the script obviously does not contain. I have entered this information where significant in the footnotes, along with my observations. Thus, this book is that very rare commodity in dramatic literature: a translation of both the printed source as well as a documented performance of the production originally directed by Dutt.

Translation

I have followed the principles of translation from Bengali that I developed for my translations of Tagore's plays first published in 1987.[21] Two of those methods require mention here: scrupulous

---

21 Rabindranath Tagore, *Three Plays* (Ananda Lal trans. and introd.; Calcutta: M P Birla Foundation, 1987; New Delhi: Oxford University Press, 2001).

fidelity to every line of text and stage direction, and adherence to spoken and colloquial language, not imposing extraneous literary rules of grammar on sentences that do not have them in the original. After all, Dutt staunchly believed in the people's idiom and conceived stage dialogue just like we speak in our everyday exchanges and conversations, often without perfect syntax or punctuation. He wrote for the actor to deliver, not for the reader to read.

The fact that Dutt composed a play in Bengali about people in Germany that I now render into English raises linguistic nuances on which a translator has to make a choice. Dutt freely used words like 'sahib', 'lakh' or 'baksheesh', part of every Indian's parlance (and life). Precisely for this reason, to make a reader in English accept *Barricade* as an *Indian* play, as *our* drama, I have kept some of these words (which already exist in common one-volume English dictionaries) rather than convert them into their Anglo-American counterparts. I find such a coinage as 'radio-wallah', with which the Justice disdainfully addresses the broadcaster, a perfect example of this Anglo-Indian hybrid, conveying associations and capturing a flavour that I must honour and express. In any case, the suffix 'wallah' has entered the *Concise Oxford Dictionary*, so we could well argue that it does not sound odd in contemporary English at all.

Other choices in vocabulary merely reflect my personal preferences, but all of them have their logic and are not arbitrary. For instance, *sramik* and *karmi* interchangeably mean 'worker', but as embedded textual clues, I have translated *sramik* as 'labourer' and *karmi* as 'worker' throughout. Bengali has two words for son, *putra* and the more informal *chhele*. Rather than render both as 'son', I converted Frau Zauritz's *chhele* for her Paul into 'boy', as an affectionate endearment for him and h.s peers, underlining the difference between her age and their youth. The Bengali *mārā* has all-purpose functionality for a wide range of meanings from 'hitting' to 'killing', so I have selected several English synonyms depending on context, instead of repeating one boringly, or indeed inaccurately. Similarly, *hāsi* means both 'laugh' and 'smile', but because we have a stage performance before us, in which smiles may go unnoticed, I have generally opted for 'laugh' in the corresponding stage directions as more apt for the theatre.

A third language enters the fray sporadically in *Barricade*. From time to time, Dutt injects German phrases and sentences to establish the illusion of authenticity. Bengali groups often apply this technique, whereby a character typically says something in English, which he or she immediately translates into Bengali even though a sizeable section of their urban audience can understand English. However, German would be incomprehensible. Nevertheless, Dutt leaves several of his German words and lines untranslated, perhaps resisting the redundancy of the prevailing method, and allows for the context or subtext or gestures to communicate their intent. I acknowledge the expertise of S. V. Raman, former Programme Director of Max Mueller Bhavan, Kolkata, in translating these faithfully for my footnotes.

Finally, I must thank Samir Majumdar, Bishnupriya Dutt and Malay Biswas, members of People's Little Theatre, for their recollections of minute details of the production that helped me to reconstruct it as best as possible. And the ever-obliging Natya Shodh Sansthan theatre archives in Kolkata for assisting me to locate contemporary reviews.

Barricade

(Based on *Unsere Strasse*—'Our Street',
a chronicle of Berlin in 1933 written by Jan Petersen)

'What is fascism? In what ways, step by step, do fascists overcast a country's skies like storm clouds? Can doctors, justices, housewives, priests, journalists, intellectuals of all kinds shut the doors of their homes and stay far from the tumult on the thoroughfares? Will fascism spare anyone? The experience of Nazi ascendancy in Germany says that in the end everyone has to come and stand at the barricades, unless it has become much too late.'[1]

Jan Petersen

---

1 Translated from Dutt's Bengali, not from Petersen's original

·

Opening night: 25 December 1972
People's Little Theatre production

Dramatis Personae

HEINRICH LANDT
(Editor and owner of *Freie Zeitung*)   Kanak Maitra

OTTO BIRKHOLZ
(Reporter of the *Freie Zeitung)*   Satya Bandyopadhyay

HERMANN STRUBBEL
(Doctor)   Mrinal Ghosh

ALBERT VOSS
(Justice)   Anil Mandal

CAPTAIN HESS
(Officer of the Detective Police)   Arun De/Pranab Pal

HITLER
(renowned)   Nirmal Bandyopadhyay

JOHANN LIPPERT
(Nazi leader)   Samir Majumdar

KURT HÜHNLEIN (HUEHNLEIN)
(Nazi Stormtrooper)   Pranab Pal

BAUER
(Nazi Stormtrooper)   Binay Gangopadhyay

MUELLER
(Nazi Stormtrooper)   Mantu Brahma

RICHARD HÜTTIG (HUETTIG)
(Communist leader)   Alok Ghoshal/
                                                 Biswanath Samanta

PAUL SCHALL
(Communist worker)   Mukul Ghosh

FRANZ ZANDER (Communist worker)	Shyamal Bhattacharya
WILLI (Communist worker)	Rajat Ghosh/Samar Nag
BRUNO (Communist worker)	Utpal Dutt/ Diptesh Bandyopadhyay
HEINZ PREUSS (Communist worker)	Pratik Ray/Malay Biswas
RUDOLF (bartender at liquor shop)	Arup Baksi
LABOURERS	Bhanu Mallik/Jnan Saha/ Ashu Saha
PROFESSOR	Santigopal Mukhopadhyay
INGEBORG ZAURITZ (wife of killed popular leader)	Sova Sen
HELGA (and) COMMUNIST WORKER[2]	Sabita Bandyopadhyay/ Snigdha Majumdar
ANNELIESE TAUSSIG (radio announcer)	Kajal Chaudhuri/ Kalyani Ray
SUTRADHAR	Nandadulal Das/ Santigopal Mukhopadhyay
BENGALI LABOURER	Biswanath Samanta/ Diptesh Bandyopadhyay

---

2 A double role, not the description of the character as suggested by the printed texts. See note 106.

Dramatization, direction and music selection	Utpal Dutt
Lighting	Tapas Sen
Scene decor	Manu Datta
Sound operation	Biswanath Samanta and Nantu Datta
Singing	Shyamal Bhattacharya
Costume design	Ayesha Khatun
Advisor	Hans Bramsche
Music	Tchaikovsky, Rossini, Wieniawski, Von Suppé,[3] David, North, Bernstein, Jarre and Prokofiev

---

3 Transliterated mistakenly in the Bengali texts as 'Phan [for Von] Juné', but Suppé's *Light Cavalry Overture* on the soundtrack of the production identifies him without any doubt.

PROLOGUE

The Sutradhar[4] comes and sings—the Red Army song: 'Comrades, the bugles are blowing!'[5] The Sutradhar is a Bengali labourer, wearing overalls. Another Bengali labourer enters, in his hand a huge spanner.

LABOURER. What's this song you're singing, Sutradhar?

SUTRADHAR. The Red Army song. The Russian labourers' army song. Revolutionary songs.

LABOURER. Why foreign songs in Kolkata? Don't you know Nazrul's[6] songs? Native revolutionary songs?

SUTRADHAR. I do. But why shouldn't I sing Red Army songs? What's native or foreign about revolutionary songs? Do you reject Europeans in revolutionary matters? I consider myself Bengali only if I can present the whole world in Kolkata's courtyard. What's in your hand?

---

4 The Sutradhār is the stage manager-cum-director of many traditional Indian theatre forms, and often appears in an opening scene to introduce the play and its main characters. Theatre need not be his profession; as in this case, he could well be a labourer or farmer.

5 In the video, the American protest ballad 'I dreamed I saw Joe Hill last night' (composed by Alfred Hayes and Earl Robinson in 1936) is sung in Bengali translation on the soundtrack before the two characters enter. Therefore, the Sutradhar does not mention the Red Army in his first two dialogues, replacing it with 'American labourers' song'. The Prologue takes place in front of the closed curtain.

6 Kazi Nazrul Islam (1899–1976), famous Bengali poet and lyricist.

LABOURER. A wrench.

SUTRADHAR. Made where?

LABOURER (*reading the name*). Made in Germany.

SUTRADHAR. It's made by German labourers. What machine do you work?

LABOURER. Springer.

SUTRADHAR. Ever bent down to see where it's made?

LABOURER. In America.

SUTRADHAR. That is, made by American labourers. When you go to war with a rifle, will you stumble around to see whether it's native stuff or not? Will you be a revolutionary outcast if you fire a foreign gun? What's in your pocket?

LABOURER (*pulls the book out*). Lenin's essay regarding trade unions.

SUTRADHAR. Foreign, foreign!

LABOURER. Smoke a biri?

SUTRADHAR. I don't smoke, hurts my throat. We're labourers, so we have no country, the earth's our country. American labourers, Tanzanian labourers, Chinese labourers and us—the same race. No difference there between European clothes and khadi.

LABOURER. What play's on today?

SUTRADHAR. Today's play will have Germany's story—Germany 1933.

LABOURER. What's the play's name?

(*Four German labourers enter with four huge posters—on the posters written respectively, DE-CA-BAR-RI*)

That's the difficulty, all these English words, can't understand their meanings. Have to go with a dictionary to watch theatre. Maybe it's not right to reject foreigners, that doesn't mean foreign words must be used anywhere and everywhere. What's decabarri? What does the word mean?

SUTRADHAR (*to the Germans*). What? Stand properly, it's going wrong.

(*The labourers rearrange themselves into: BARRICADE.*)

LABOURER. Oh, barricade, say so.

SUTRADHAR. Although barricade's a foreign word too. But all the workmen on the planet know the word's meaning, because when you have to fight by blocking roads with dustbins, pipes and bricks, New York's Harlem and Kolkata's Khidirpur become one.

LABOURER. Sutradhar, the actors and actresses who'll perform this drama are capable, right? What are the characters in the play?

(*As the curtain rises, Otto, Landt, Lippert, Strubbel, Voss, Ingeborg show themselves in the shape of cartoons.*[7])

LIPPERT. Heil Hitler!

SUTRADHAR. What's your name? Your profession?

LIPPERT. Johann Lippert. I'm an ordinary worker of the Nazi Party, Standartenfuehrer of the SS Unit. We want to construct socialism in war-devastated, confused Germany under the great Hitler's leadership.

LABOURER. What does the word Nazi mean?

LIPPERT. You can say the word Nazi is our party's nickname. The full name is Nationalsozialistische Arbeiterpartei, that is, nationalistic socialistic workers' group. We'll construct socialism by the genuine German method, not on the basis of some borrowed foreign principles.

---

7 These 'cartoons' take the form of cardboard cutouts in the video, with openings through which they place their heads and hands.

STRUBBEL. There we go again. The risk of moving about on Berlin roads in 1933 created by politics. I'm Hermann Strubbel.

SUTRADHAR. Profession?

STRUBBEL. Doctor. But it's become impossible to go out to practise.

SUTRADHAR. Why?

STRUBBEL. Battling on the streets—Nazis against Communists. So I don't come out any more. Sit at home and read books.

LABOURER. What do you read? Medical books?

STRUBBEL. Are you mad? Schopenhauer, Hegel, Kant. All nineteenth-century books. I don't read anything of this age, I don't need this age.

LANDT (*on the phone*). The reporters' desk—get it quick.

SUTRADHAR. Will you introduce yourself?

LANDT. Oh, what a pain. My name's Heinrich Landt, I'm editor— and owner—of Germany's largest-circulated impartial news-paper, *Freie Zeitung*.[8] Don't disturb me, I'm doing urgent work.

OTTO (*lifts the phone*). Hello.

LANDT. Birkholz? Leave immediately. Go to the Presidential man-sion. The President has called for Adolf Hitler. Something big's about to happen—go quick.

LIPPERT. Heil Hitler! Our victory's imminent.

STRUBBEL. Quiet, quiet.

OTTO (*on the phone*). I just returned with news of the Communist Party meeting.

LANDT (*on the phone*). You have to come out again. Aren't you a reporter? Reporter for the *Freie Zeitung* paper?

---

8 Fictitious. Switzerland, not Germany, had a newspaper titled *Freie Zeitung*, but it appeared from 1917 to 1920.

OTTO. I've realized that seventeen dead donkeys make one reporter . . . that donkey's named 'Reporter'.

SUTRADHAR (*to Voss*). Sir, you seem like a big shot. May I be introduced to you?

VOSS. What right do you have to be introduced to me?

SUTRADHAR. I'm the Sutradhar, in charge of stringing this play together—

VOSS. I'm Albert Voss, Justice.

SUTRADHAR. Oh my! A Judge sahib!

VOSS. Therefore I see no necessity to talk with people on the road.

SUTRADHAR. Forgive us, Your Honour, I only wanted to know, these political killings going on in Germany every day—

VOSS. I don't know or understand politics. If you kill, I punish you in court, but I don't let politics enter the court.

STRUBBEL. I don't let politics enter even my study. Only in procuring knowledge is there no politics.

SUTRADHAR (*to Inge*). What do you say?

INGE. I too don't understand politics.

SUTRADHAR. Your introduction?

INGE. What introduction? I've no introduction, a common person, homemaker, my name's Ingeborg. However, you may have heard my husband's name—Josef Zauritz.

SUTRADHAR. Yes, yes, a generous hero, a people's leader respected by all.

INGE. His introduction is mine. However, we're not in all that political slaughter.

STRUBBEL. Absolutely not.

VOSS. Not at all.

LANDT. Impartial, unafraid newspapers can never get tangled in political factionalism.

LABOURER. Is this ever possible? Can politics be prohibited from entry by closing the doors of a house?

INGE. It can. It has to. Our adopted son Paul Schall has become a Communist, a fugitive from the neighbourhood. Seeing his vagabond, violent looks has made me understand all the more that we have to stay away from politics.

VOSS. A Justice has no politics—

STRUBBEL. An intellectual has no politics—

LANDT. A newspaper has no politics—

INGE. A common person has no politics—

LIPPERT. No politics is higher than the homeland—

(*All of them become invisible.*[9])

LABOURER. You're all making a mistake. Born in Karl Marx's country, should you ever say: I have no politics? The tumult on the roads never reaches my ears? I'm blind and deaf?

SUTRADHAR. Hey idiot, think of your own story, worry about your own homeland. You don't have to worry about the German population in 1933. Yes, once they were on the heights of dreamland, when barricades lay on the avenues. No more wasting words then, spending time in vain, the actors are prepared—let the play begin—there's the reporter from the *Freie Zeitung* paper returning from the Presidential mansion to the office—

---

9 In the video, the curtain closes on them (leaving the Sutradhar and Labourer outside as before), and remains closed for Scene One which takes place in front of it.

ONE

OTTO.[10] 'Therefore, at 10.15 this morning, invited by the President, the Nazi Party leader, Adolf Hitler, was instated with the full powers of Chancellor and Prime Minister.' I've realized that seventeen donkeys, after dying, make one reporter for a newspaper. One who silently bears on his back History's heavy packages, who fills his stomach by eating the leftovers from various political groups, who has no necessity for either sleep or rest, on whose back falls incessantly the rods of various owners, that donkey's name is Reporter. (*Taking a bottle out of the desk, has a gulp of liquor*) There's nothing called a work bell in the journalist's profession. The pressures of night duty make one's wife a stranger. After doing duty for ten nights at a stretch, I got leave early last morning. Early means two at night. Reaching home at three, I enter the bedroom, the wife says in a sleepy voice, 'Who, is it Karl?' I was really shocked—because my name's not Karl, it's Otto. Otto Birkholz. My wife can't not know this. Now who's this Karl, why's there a possibility of him stepping into my wife's bedroom at three in the night, why does my wife not feel startled seeing a strange male

---

10 After entering, Otto drapes his coat over the back of a chair, takes a liquor bottle out from its pocket and puts it on the table. He does not take it out of the desk as the stage direction indicates later. Then he reads from a notebook.

named Karl in her room late at night but asks after him adroitly?—I never found the time to solve all these mysteries. I came back to join work, because at 10.15 in the morning today, 30 January 1933, Hitler became Prime Minister of Germany.

(*Somewhere in the distance bombs burst, bullets fly.*)

There it starts again. A war continues between Nazis and Communists on the roads of Berlin. In the past six months 461 skirmishes took place with pistols, bombs, knives and beer bottles. In one month, 83[11] political killings took place in this city. Everyone's protecting wives, sons, family; people don't walk on Berlin's avenues after dark. Except one reporter. He's everywhere. To write a chronicle of demolition, for the past one year I've had to go into unapproachable alleys where bombs burst on all sides, the wide crossroads of Unter den Linden where some newly murdered political worker lies sprawled, the central police lockup where a hundred-odd students are given severe floggings with rubber batons, Nazi Stormtrooper[12] processions where bombs burst and bullets fly at every step. I see all this and feel my pulse to see whether the life I inherited is there or not!

(*Once again, coming from the distance, the noise of bombs and tumult.*)

This is a very odd country. Elections are held incessantly here. Germany has had five elections in three years. Elections were

---

11 The number was 86 in the first edition.

12 The Sturmabteilung, the Nazi paramilitary forces. During this speech in the video, the curtain has opened, and, after this sentence, a choreographed mime commences of Nazis oppressing a woman, then facing Communist workers who enter. A battle and shootout occur. The curtain closes again for the rest of this scene.

held on 14 September 1930. At which, of 608 seats in the legislative assembly,[13] Hitler's Nazi Party got 107 and the labourers' parties got 350. Naturally, 107 is greater than 350; so the President called on Hitler to form the council of ministers. But people don't understand mathematics. When they went mad and started trouble, the legislative assembly was dissolved and elections held again in March 1932.[14] Again Hitler lost. So the legislative assembly was dissolved once more, elections once more on 10 April 1932, and Hitler lost once more. Then once more the legislative assembly was dissolved, once more elections on 31 July 1932. This time the Nazi Party got 230 seats, the labourers' parties 222. But the small groups created trouble; all gathered in the shadow of the Communist Party umbrella. As a result, against 230 Nazis in the legislative assembly stood 378 members of various parties.[15] Therefore the urgent necessity of defending democracy showed itself again. On 30 August, at the legislative

---

13 The Reichstag. In fact, it had 577 seats in 1930. The number increased to 608 for the July 1932 elections.

14 Germany held presidential (*not* legislative) elections in two rounds in March–April 1932, which President-incumbent Hindenburg won, defeating Hitler.

15 However, the smaller parties did not see eye to eye, as a result of which a majority coalition government could not form. In fact, the two main leftist parties, the Social Democratic Party and the Communist Party, had traditionally never agreed, and it was largely because of their apparently irreconcilable differences that the Nazi Party could take over gradually. Dutt turned an essentially tripartite power tussle into a right–left binary, so as to draw the audience's attention to the analogous politics in West Bengal, where the socialistic United Front government wrangled and imploded twice, virtually allowing the Congress to wrest control in 1972.

assembly's first session, the sitting assembly was annulled[16] and elections once more—6 November 1932. This time the Nazis got 196 seats, the labourers' parties 221. And when the other groups supported the Communist Party, the position in the legislative assembly stood at—Nazi 196, anti-Nazi 412.[17] Now even a schoolchild knows that 196 is greater than 412. So at 10.15 in the morning today, the leader of those 196, Hitler, has been made Prime Minister, and the legislative assembly has been dissolved to fix elections again, once more, encore, next March 5. This time Hitler will oversee the elections as Prime Minister—

(*Tremendous explosion.*)

—there, he's doing it! Actually you can't have democracy just by shouting it's a democracy. You have to understand what's democracy. So long as the Communists aren't thoroughly evicted from the legislative assembly, the assembly will be dissolved, there'll be election after election—that's it. (*Drinks liquor*) Now if the foolish men of this country go on voting for the Communists, elections will turn into a permanent annual ritual like weddings, funerals, divorces and so on. We'll know that democracy's established only when the Nazi Party grabs 608 out of 608 seats in the legislative assembly—not otherwise.

(*Landt enters with excited steps, his hair a dazzling grey from age, wearing costly clothes, the chain of a gold watch clearly visible on his waistcoat.*[18])

---

16 Actually it was dissolved in September.

17 412 is wrong, because seats had decreased to 584 in this election. But the Nazis were disappointed that they won only 196, compared to their previous result.

18 He sits down in the video.

LANDT. Well, Otto, you're here?

OTTO (*rising*). Where else would I go, sir?

LANDT. Sit, sit. I have some terrible news. You'll collect a full account of it, including interview. More than one interview. You'll write it properly, after meeting all individuals involved—written for the front page, daily for fifteen days. (*Springs to lift the phone*) Get me Stein.

OTTO. You'll give my life insurance premium, Herr Landt, for if I have to move around on Berlin's roads I don't know whether I'll return.

LANDT (*on the phone*). Stein? Landt speaking. What's the top headline on tomorrow's front page? Remove all that. Stuff it on another page, empty that space. No, no, the Soviet Red Army isn't entering Germany, you know it, I know it. There is no cause to fill the front page with all those hoaxes. Otto Birkholz is writing what's going instead. You'll get the full matter by two at night, with pictures. (*Puts the phone down.*)

OTTO. Meaning I'll toil till two?

LANDT. Yes. If you hear the news you won't object any more. Otto, Josef Zauritz[19] has been killed.

(*Silence*)

OTTO. Zauritz? Impossible.

---

19 The real Josef Zauritz (1897–1933) was a police officer in Charlottenburg, shot dead on the night of 30 January 1933 in front of Wallstrasse 24, while monitoring a triumphant Nazi procession there after Hitler's appointment as Chancellor. He was one of the first two to be killed after Hitler came to power. Local revolutionary workers claimed him as their friend. In 1965, the case was reopened and it was found that a Stormtrooper had shot both men.

LANDT. Killed. In broad daylight—three in the afternoon. In Wallstrasse, on the street in front of his house.

OTTO. An old patriot aged 70, he had no enemies—can't have enemies—

LANDT. He does. They knifed him and went away leaving the bloody corpse behind.

OTTO. Who are they?

LANDT (*after a moment's silence*). The Communists.

OTTO. Their gain in murdering an old man of 70?

LANDT (*standing up in tremendous excitement*). Gain? Gain? Since when have they done anything after calculating worldly gains or losses? Who made our lives unendurable over the last 15 years? Who first brought the politics of killing? Not the Communists in 1918?

OTTO. Of course.

LANDT. Liebknecht and Rosa Luxemburg[20] were the first to commence this bloodshed by firing the first bullets. Since then, this . . . this perdition of ours continues.

OTTO. But I'd heard that the Communists respected Zauritz.

LANDT. In a speech last week, Zauritz condemned the Communists' violent work. So this wrath. Of course, this too is a secondary cause. Actually this is, in their perverted language, the red terror. Widening the path to grab power by devastating people's lives through any means.

OTTO. Your language is gradually taking the shape of our paper's editorials.

---

20 Karl Liebknecht (1871–1919) and Rosa Luxemburg (1871–1919), cofounders of the Communist Party of Germany.

LANDT (*laughing gently*). I'm the editor, it's fine that I'm not speaking through the headlines. You should leave now. The dead body's in the morgue, if you want to see once—

OTTO (*as if frightened*). No, no, there's not much point in questioning a dead body. Dead bodies don't give statements. And even if they do, it's about otherworldly topics, can't be printed in this paper.

LANDT. Captain Hess of the Detective Police is investigating, meet him and get to know the whole incident. Besides, the eyewitness to this killing was Josef Zauritz's elderly wife.

OTTO. What?

LANDT. That's what I heard. Meet her. Give a language to Berlin's anger by dipping your pen in her tears.

OTTO. Her address?

LANDT. The actual address is 116 Wallstrasse, Charlottenburg Borough, Berlin. But now she's under police guard at No. 10 Friedrichstrasse.

OTTO (*while writing it*). Who gave you the news?

LANDT. The Nazi Party leader, Lippert. Besides, at midnight, the Police Minister himself will give a radio broadcast regarding this . . . this abominable, bestial, dehumanized homicide.

OTTO. You're editorializing again! Half of it can't be understood.

LANDT (*momentarily irritated*). This is a newspaper office. I had hopes that everyone here will at least learn the German language well. (*Springs to lift the phone*) Get me Stein. (*To Otto*) Lippert is giving an election speech today. At Sportpalast. If you leave immediately, you can catch him there. (*On the phone*) Stein? Hear what will be tomorrow's headline—banner spread over five columns—'Communists dance on avenue after brutally murdering old popular leader aged 80'. Written it down? Fine. Otto's writing the story. (*Puts the phone down.*)

OTTO. Look, it's not an intelligent thing to decide the story's title before reading the story. When my wife got pregnant last year, we jointly decided to name the boy Friedrich. But a girl was born. Friedrich can't be a girl's name, after all.

LANDT. There's no scope for that sort of mishap here.

OTTO. Sure there is. You say 'Communists dance on avenue'. How did you know? Were you there or what? You saw them dancing with red flags?

LANDT. Even if they didn't dance, you'll make them dance by the force of your pen. You'll keep my headline's honour.

OTTO. What's the proof that the Communists slew him?

LANDT. Hah! Mrs Zauritz saw it with her own eyes, the police caught a Communist leader red-handed, lots more proof. To assemble them all is your evening tryst. Go, leave.

OTTO. Your headline has more mistakes. You say, 'old popular leader aged 80'. But Zauritz's age is 70.

LANDT. At 80, the tragedy's more lasting. (*Something strikes his mind and he lifts the phone again*) Get me Stein. (*To Otto*) There's no doubt that the Communists slew him. The Nazis kill too, but Josef Zauritz was revered by Hitler himself. The Nazis can't have laid hands on him. Who remains? Those Communists. (*On the phone*) Stein? Write it down, banner on top, 80-year-old, etcetera, Communists dance, etcetera—then second heading, not less than 36-point—'Husband's warm blood coats wife's body'. Written? *Sehr gut.*[21] (*Puts phone down.*)

---

21 'Very well.' (Dutt uses German phrases and sentences occasionally.)

OTTO. This creates another inconvenience. Why did they spill blood on the elderly lady's body? How will I pack all this into the report—

LANDT. Hah! An elderly lady eyewitness. Drops of blood can splatter her.

OTTO. Where was the elderly lady? From where did she become an eyewitness? Suppose she witnessed the killing from a first-floor window, then what will I write? The Communists cupped the blood and threw it upwards? Or brought a pump and hose like a fire engine to throw blood—

LANDT. Wherever she saw it from, you'll bring her onto the street. Then write a fearful description of Mrs Zauritz smeared by husband's blood. (*Slamming his fist on the table*) The Communists must be finished. (*Controlling himself, moves, not too far*) You know, Otto, those who have teenagers or young men at home can't go to sleep at night anymore? The Communists have made killings, riots, beheadings so easy that today men swallow 10 or 12 daily killings like their morning coffee. The race's sense of morals and values is crumbling. The values of life are crumbling down like an insolvent bank. No incident can be more unfeeling than this. Cracks show up in the foundation of civilization. The Nazis have many faults but the Communists are a manifest curse. You leave, take the car. I want the write-up by two.

OTTO. It won't be done by two. I'll have to meet many people, have to go home once too—otherwise that mysterious individual named Karl might attack my bedroom.

LANDT. Have you drunk too much liquor? You're delirious.

OTTO. In short, it isn't possible to complete writing the thrilling history by two at night.

LANDT (*laughing*). Everything can happen if you toil. God built the entire earth in six days.

OTTO. Have you looked at the earth lately? Can you say that it's been built very well? I have the impression that God, in his hurry, botched the matter into this.

LANDT. Get up, get to work. *Das ist ein Befehl.*[22] I order you. (*Otto goes ahead with slow, unwilling steps.*) Otto, look at me. (*Takes the gold watch out from his pocket*) What's this?

OTTO. A watch, that much German I know.

LANDT. This watch you, the employees of this paper, had given me one day. Remember?

OTTO. Don't I remember? Everyone had to give 300 marks from their salary. As a result, my quantity of liquor that month was cut to half.

LANDT. Why did you give this watch?

OTTO. It was needed to keep the editor pleased. Otherwise our jobs would go.

LANDT. Don't joke, look—what had you written on the back of the watch? (*Reads*) 'To our editor Heinrich Landt, who is not afraid to tell the truth.' Do you still have that belief in Heinrich Landt?

OTTO. If I didn't, would I still do this damned job?

LANDT (*in a proud yet calm voice*). Otto Birkholz, I touch this watch and say, I am not and will not be afraid to tell the truth. I will uncover the Communist conspiracy and spread it out in front

---

22 'That is an order.' (Rarely, Dutt translates his German usages immediately in Bengali, as in this instance. However, since he does not always translate literally, I have provided accurate translations in the footnotes whenever his translated dialogues differ slightly.)

of the populace. Not for fear of anyone, but in the interest of truth, in the interest of our newspaper's ideals. Now go to Sportpalast. Lippert is giving a speech there.

TWO

At Sportpalast, in front of massive flags bearing swastikas and illuminated by dazzling white lights, Lippert sahib is speechifying at top voice in front of a row of mikes. The stage for the speech is guarded by a few armed members of the Stormtroopers.[23]

LIPPERT. The helpless, unarmed, respected-by-all, patriotic people's leader Josef Zauritz was then about to get into the car. Suddenly a group of villains encircled him, red badges on their arms and slogans on their lips: 'Victory to the Communist Party!' Eleven times—eleven times they stabbed him, cut the old man's thin body to pieces and flew the victory pennant of egalitarianism. They fulfilled their revenge by murdering the husband in front of the elderly wife's eyes. The Josef Zauritz who tolerated endless persecution for the country since 1901, was killed by a group of political goons whose country is actually not Germany but the Soviet Union. If you don't believe my words, go to the Charlottenburg police office. The police arrested an individual carrying a bloody knife within two hours of the incident from a secret hideout nearby. You know who he is? The Communist Party's Charlottenburg District Secretary, Richard Huettig. (*Sounds of loud jeering from the people*) Will you still let this politics of killing continue? (*Sounds of 'No, no' from the people*) Evict the killer goons of the Communist Party by the force of votes next March 5. (*Joyous*

---

23 The curtain opens for this scene.

sounds) To establish peace and order, we have to fight as one life, one race behind one leader, that leader is Adolf Hitler. (*Joyous sounds*) Our party is the Nazi Party. That is, the National Socialist Party. That is, both nationalism and socialism are our mantras. Germany has to be built into a fortress of nationalism, we have to make the great leader's hands strong, Germany has to be guided towards socialism. Socialism is coming under Adolf Hitler's leadership. Vote for the Nazi Party. Sieg Heil!

(*Amid loud, joyous sounds, Lippert descends from the stage, wipes his face with a hanky. The Stormtroopers had surrounded him and were taking him away, at which time Otto arrives.*)

OTTO. Herr Lippert! Standartenfuehrer Lippert.

KURT (*leader of the Stormtroopers*). What do you want? Herr Lippert's tired, has to go to another meeting.

OTTO. I've come on behalf of the *Freie Zeitung* paper, I want an interview urgently. Five minutes or so.

KURT. Interview on what matter?

OTTO. The Zauritz murder. The editor, Heinrich Landt, sent me.

(*Lippert turns round and looks.*)

LIPPERT. Kurt, let him come.

MUELLER. *Ausweis?*[24] Let's see your press card.

(*Otto shows it, and after that, at a sign from Mueller, goes ahead to Lippert.*)

LIPPERT. Please don't mind these boys' strictness. They've become anxious about my safety after seeing the Communists' actions.

---

24 'ID?'

OTTO. Quite natural. However, tell your bodyguard there's no necessity to lay hands on people from the start. My shoulder's aching.

(*Everyone laughs uproariously.*)

KURT. Sorry. Will you drink some coffee?

OTTO. No beer?

(*The Stormtrooper boys shudder.*)

LIPPERT (*laughing*). Our leader Hitler doesn't drink liquor, nor eats fish and meat. He's vegetarian. So nobody in our party touches liquor. However, there's no bar on bringing it for you. Bauer—

OTTO. No, no, there's no need. (*Looking at the boys this time with an appreciative gaze*) Many people say many indecent things about you. But now I see—

LIPPERT. They are the future of the race. Take this Kurt Huehnlein. A successful university student. His father's a millionaire. Yet he's toiling as a whole-time worker of our party at a daily salary of only five marks. This Mueller is a labourer's son. Earlier, he was in the Anarchist Party. Now he believes in and fights for our doctrines and ideals. A millionaire's son and a labourer's son, in our party—

KURT (*looking at his watch*). There's not much time, though.

LIPPERT (*laughing*). See how strict he is! I'm going, I'm going. Yes, tell me, what do you want to know? (*Suddenly his facial muscles start to quiver violently, he holds his face tightly*[25]) Oof!

KURT. Chair, chair!

---

[25] In the video, at the first manifestation, Otto quickly moves away from Lippert to safety.

(*Bauer brings a chair, Lippert sits. Kurt gives water, offers a medicine pill. Lippert swallows it.*)

LIPPERT. I'm unwell. Please don't mind. You see this side of my face trembling, I've no power over it. I have no control. It starts trembling suddenly.

OTTO. Then I'd better—

LIPPERT. No, no, it'll be fine soon.

KURT. It's the impossible hard work. Three or four public assemblies in a day.

LIPPERT. Actually from much earlier—incessant jail, torture, hard work since '23—my constitution broke down.

MUELLER. For the country.

OTTO. That's what I say. You've done so much for the country. This time you need rest, so this time I've decided to vote for the Communists.

(*Everyone is startled. Lippert laughs out, the boys[26] join him.*)

LIPPERT. Not a bad idea. Yes, tell me, what's your question?

OTTO. How was the Communist leader Huettig arrested?

LIPPERT. Police sniffer dogs entered a house. The police found a bloodstained knife there after a search, and some garments— also with bloody marks.

OTTO. Where's Huettig now?

LIPPERT. In the lockup.

OTTO. When's the trial?

LIPPERT. That depends on the Justice, Albert Voss. However, Voss will begin preliminary hearings and investigations day after

---

26 And Otto, too, in the video.

tomorrow. If you show up there, you'll get to know everything. Room Number 6 in the High Court.

OTTO. What do you think? Are the Communists truly responsible?

LIPPERT (*laughs*). As a Nazi I'll say—certainly.

OTTO. And as an intelligent man?

BAUER. You want to say that Nazis are ignorant?

(*Lippert and Kurt laugh.*)

LIPPERT. As a citizen I'll say—as far as available proof goes, I think the Communist Party has done the killing, but we cannot be certain yet.

OTTO. What proof has been found other than the knife and clothes?

LIPPERT. The police chief smiled and said some leaflets had been found. Another witness has been found at the scene of the incident—Dr Strubbel or Staubbel, some such name. Besides, there's Mrs Zauritz's testimony.

OTTO. Has that lady identified Huettig?

LIPPERT. That'll be in front of Voss at the time of the hearing. Now the lady's almost speechless from sorrow. And our party's dumbfounded too. You know, even at this time the lady has no respite. She's being pressured to give a radio broadcast, to give a statement, to pay Hitler a visit. And the police had virtually dragged her out, forcibly. As party representative of this locality, I was compelled to stop all that monkey business. I've issued strict orders that no one should disturb the lady. I won't tolerate the baseness of using her as a pawn in the elections.

OTTO. One more question—will the Communist Party be declared illegal?

LIPPERT. Illegal! Why?

OTTO. Since they killed Zauritz.

LIPPERT.[27] The National Socialist Party doesn't believe in all that oppression. Our leader Adolf Hitler will confront the Communists in independent and unobstructed elections—next 5 March. We won't tolerate the Communist Party's slightest interference in democratic rights. This isn't Russia. We won't allow Stalin's repressive methods here. We'll build socialism on a different path, the path of peace and order. We didn't and won't let them arrest anybody but Huettig. The police wanted to arrest—catch everyone in one swoop on the Communist Party office of Charlottenburg. We didn't let them.

KURT. Herr Standartenfuehrer! Don't get excited.

LIPPERT (*not listening to him*). The police wanted to catch Zauritz's adopted son, Paul Schall. He's a Communist Party member.

OTTO (*while writing*). Paul Schall . . . adopted son . . .

LIPPERT. Yes, the Zauritzes raised him. The police feel that boy let his party leader Huettig know when Zauritz left his house, when he could be murdered unopposed. But we didn't let him be arrested, though nobody else may know the cause, I know. Mrs Zauritz loves Paul so much. The husband's gone, will they snatch the boy from her breast now, to kill the elderly lady too? (*Begins to quiver violently, Kurt and others hold him.*) We aren't capable of such great cruelty. Politics by abandoning humanity—I'm not capable of it. I have to go, Herr Birkholz, there's another meeting. Look—don't go and disturb that grief-stricken, widowed, companionless elderly lady.[28]

---

27 In the video, Lippert screams the first words out so suddenly that Otto's notebook, in which he has been writing ever since Lippert had his convulsions, goes flying from his hands. Otto catches it on the way down while Lippert continues speaking.

28 The curtains close for the next scene, which takes place in front.

THREE

Ingeborg Zauritz sits in a room covered in darkness in her house. In her grey tresses over black mourning dress, she is a living image of world-weary loneliness. Arrangements for tea on a table in front. On the other side, another chair—empty. Ingeborg is pouring tea for two and saying many things to her invisible life-partner, as if filling her companionless reality with her imagination.

INGE. Where will you go today, Josef? . . . Do you have to go towards the orphanage? I hear there's fighting that side every day . . . I know you need to inspect schools, orphanages, hospitals every day, but don't be late, understand? You need rest too. You're getting old. (*Silence*) Josef, I have to buy some ties for you. I saw them yesterday at a shop in Alexanderplatz. Yes, the money for expenses you gave me will last out this month. . . . Cigar? Want a cigar? (*Getting up, she brings cigars and matches and puts them on the hand-rest of the armchair.*) Tell the driver to stock up on petrol. The times are such—

(*Paul has entered secretively, and listens to her delirious talk.*)

What's this? Why are your shoes so dirty? No, no, I'll polish them. I won't let you leave the house in this manner. (*Sits on the carpet and pretends to clean shoes.*) What will people say? (*Laughs*) They'll say at this advanced age our love has decreased. Otherwise why doesn't the old woman see to all this! (*As soon as she raises her face, she sees Paul behind the chair. Extremely embarrassed, she stands up very slowly.*) Paul! Paul, when did you come? How, here—won't they catch you?

PAUL. No, Mother. You . . . you're absolutely alone, aren't you?

INGE. Your looks have worsened. You don't sleep at night, do you?

PAUL. I don't lie down in the same house for two nights running, that's why.

INGE. Will you eat anything?

PAUL. No. How's your health?

INGE. Not bad.

PAUL. When will you bury Father?

INGE. Don't know. As it is that body's cut to pieces. On top of that they're cutting it into long slices with knives in the name of an autopsy. Even the dignity of death wasn't in his fate. (*Paul had sat on the empty chair; Inge says in an enraged tone*) Don't sit there, stand up.

PAUL (*stands up*). Mother, Father is no more, you have to accept this truth—otherwise you'll go mad.

INGE. And I don't have a boy, this truth too I have to accept—isn't that so?

PAUL. What are you saying, Mother?

INGE. I'm accusing—you're connected with this killing too. Are your politics satisfied by drinking blood this time? Are you at peace after gulping Josef Zauritz's blood?

PAUL. Unjust—you're being unjust! Why are you talking like this to me? Have I killed Father?

INGE. Not with your own hand, perhaps. Your party has. Your dear leader and friend Huettig slew him with his own hands.

PAUL. This is not true.

INGE. I saw it with my own eyes. Heard with my own ears their violent shouts. They were shouting with happiness after sacrificing Josef Zauritz.

PAUL (*forcefully*). Mother, don't believe the enemy's words. The Communist Party doesn't kill furtively. Father was—(*As Inge laughs out hoarsely, Paul stops.*) Why are you laughing?

INGE. Hearing your words—'The Communist Party doesn't kill furtively.' It's not even ten days, didn't all of you drag out Ludwig Meissner from the house on the corner and kill him? My eyes are bad—perhaps I won't be able to recognize in court who slew my husband. But didn't Huettig kill Meissner? (*Paul does not answer.*) You don't reply, so I understand my husband had guessed right. I have another question: Were you among those who slew Meissner?

(*Silence*)

PAUL. Yes I was. Hear some more—I stabbed him too. You're my mother, so I'm telling you, Ludwig Meissner was a goon, the owner's agent. Sheltered by the police, he killed five of our comrades.

INGE. I don't believe it. He was a young boy of 22, moving about on the streets, in pain from unemployment. We picked you up from the road and raised you, otherwise what's the difference between you and Meissner?

PAUL. He joined the Nazis' group.

INGE. Because his stomach ached with hunger. Anyway, it's been admitted that you people kill furtively.

PAUL. Out of necessity, but it's not our custom.

INGE. There's such a divide between necessity and custom among you?

PAUL (*striding around the room*). Mother, you're a God-fearing Catholic. How will you understand my words? For you believe in the life supreme and sacred.

INGE. So you people don't call life sacred?

PAUL. There's nothing that's supreme or ultimate, there's no purity detached from the earth's conflicts. We don't see life separately from class struggle. One war continues. In this war, when the owner has a labourer killed, it's a crime. But when the labourer murders the owner's pet goon as a reply to 300 years of exploitation, it's self-defence, it's justice. A bigger question than whether life's sacred or not is: Who's taking whose life?

INGE. So you not only killed Meissner, you're also happy that you killed him.

PAUL. Yes—I'm happy I've repaid the debt for my five dead comrades. I'm happy I've defended the lives of all those other comrades whom Meissner would have killed.

INGE. Then perhaps Josef Zauritz, too, you . . . (*Looks at Paul with a horrified gaze*) Were you in that group too?

PAUL. Listen, listen, you're making a mistake—we didn't slay Father, he—

INGE. Not Father, Josef Zauritz. You stabbed him in the chest?

PAUL (*forcefully*). Why? Why stab him?

INGE. Because you detested him all your life.

(*Paul is nonplussed as if caught unprepared.*)

PAUL (*in an idly excited voice*). How did you get to know that I detested him all my life? Was it expressed in my behaviour?

INGE. Not in your behaviour, in your eyes. You used to detest him.

PAUL. Yes, I used to. I used to detest him for lifting me up from the road and giving me shelter. I can't tolerate any debts to anyone. He didn't give me birth, he gave me kindness and compassion. Such great audacity—he'll give alms to men. Distribute from above. He who got and he who gave, how would the two unite? Well, I never thought of you as Frau Zauritz, friend of the poor. I always thought of you as Mother.[29]

---

29 In the video, Paul comes to Inge and holds her.

INGE (*a little later, in a calm and steady voice*). Kindly leave this house and go away, never come back. As a God-fearing Christian, I should have forgiven all of you. But I can't do it. Now go away. (*Paul sets out.*) Where's Clara? The girl you used to love—rather, said you loved. I've doubts whether you can love anyone at all. Clara's well, I hope?

PAUL. I've heard she's well, I haven't seen her for many days. I've heard she's walking about again.

INGE. Walking about? What happened to her?

PAUL. The Nazis hit her terribly. As she's Communist too.

(*Paul exits. Inge stays sitting motionless for a while.*)

INGE (*in a tired tone*). Josef, there are battles in this city day and night. Come, let's go away somewhere else.

(*Otto enters fearfully.*)

OTTO. Frau Zauritz!

INGE (*not startled at all*). What do you want? Who are you?

OTTO. I come on behalf of the *Freie Zeitung* paper—

INGE. How did you enter this house?

OTTO. Secretly. Can I ask one or two questions?

INGE. I'm tired. Tired of questions.

OTTO. Won't you let our huge readership know of the incident? Shouldn't people know?

INGE (*after thinking a little*). At first I thought I'd stay quiet, keeping my sorrows to myself. But I understood from their words that if I don't hold their hands down immediately, they'll kill many others on the pretext of their class struggle. Ask what questions you will. (*Otto goes to sit on the empty chair*) But you can't sit there.

OTTO. Oh, so you believe in ghosts? I do too.

INGE. Meaning?

OTTO. It's all right, I'll sit on the floor. (*Takes a seat.*)

INGE. You haven't closed the door tight. It's terribly cold outside. Close the door.

OTTO (*after staring bewildered for some time*). Door? If the door's closed, will the outside become warm?

(*A faint trace of a smile can be seen on Inge's face.*)

INGE. You're quite a wit. I had the impression newspaper people were down-to-earth, excitable, short-tempered, quarrelsome.

OTTO. You're talking about my wife.

(*This time Inge laughs for a moment.*)

INGE. Ask what you will.

OTTO. I don't wish to ask, because you'll feel sad in replying. Nevertheless I'm compelled to speak in the interest of the populace's demands, the newspaper's independence, democracy's victory, and all fearful things, etcetera. Are you truly an eyewitness to the homicide?[30]

INGE. Yes.

OTTO. Where were you?

INGE. At the door. The car was on that side of the road.[31] My husband said goodbye and went to that side of the road to get into the car. He just opened the door—

OTTO. Then what happened?

---

30 He begins taking notes in the video.

31 Here, in the video, Otto interjects, 'Oh, then the blood couldn't have splattered on your body . . . Okay, let that be,' and then stops himself. Inge continues her speech and Otto goes back to recording in his notebook.

INGE. A car came and braked in the middle of the road. Five people jumped down from it. They surrounded my husband!

OTTO. What were they wearing?

INGE. Very ordinary workingmen's clothes, caps on their heads. But on each one's left arm a red badge was shining.

OTTO. They surrounded Zauritz. Then?

INGE. Couldn't see clearly because, remember, this was occurring on that side of a couple of cars. It appeared a scuffle was going on.

OTTO. Weren't the killers shouting?

INGE. Yes—they shouted, 'Long live the Communist Party', and 'Red Front'.

OTTO. What did you do?

INGE. It seemed my legs were joined to the doorframe. I couldn't move, shouts weren't splitting my throat open. I stood there, watching them kill my husband.

OTTO. Frau Zauritz, these recollections are making you sad, so—

INGE. I'm not sad at all. The inside's become benumbed. Tell me, what else do you want to know?

OTTO. Did you see Richard Huettig in this group?

INGE. I can't say I recognized him. My eyes are bad. On top of that, the incident occurred behind two cars.

OTTO. Do you know Huettig?

INGE. Certainly. I know all the Communist boys in this neighbourhood. Huettig was an object of dear affection for my husband.

OTTO. Then why would they slay him?

INGE. About ten days ago, a boy named Meissner was killed in this neighbourhood. My husband guessed it was the Communists' work and even gave a statement condemning them. Since then, a divide sprang up between Huettig and him.

OTTO. But you didn't see Huettig in the killers' group?

INGE. You can't say I didn't see him either. Huettig's a tall boy. Behind the cars, one person's head rose above all. I can't say for certain that he wasn't Huettig either.

OTTO. Then what did they do?

INGE. They ran back and got into the car.

OTTO. Other than red badges and slogans, did anything else make you understand they were Communists?

INGE. Yes. When they talked to one another, they used the word 'comrade'.

OTTO (*momentarily excited*). Truly?

INGE. Yes.

OTTO. What exactly were they saying? Do you remember one or two words?

INGE (*rubbing her hand on her forehead*). Everything's hazy, unclear, it appeared what was occurring wasn't true, couldn't be.

OTTO. It'd be very good if you could recall a couple of words.

INGE. Um . . . yes, like—after getting in the car, the driver asked the boy beside him, 'Where's that corner? Which way do I turn?' He used the word 'comrade' then.

OTTO. Say it in his language. What did he say?

INGE. He said, '*Wo muss ich einbiegen, Kamerad?*'[32]

OTTO. You heard clearly—'*Kamerad*'. Then?

---

32 'Where should I turn, comrade?'

INGE. The car went away. Then I saw Dr Strubbel come out from the clinic next door and bend over that bloodstained mass of flesh that had been my husband just a little while before.

OTTO. You couldn't take down the killers' car number, certainly.

INGE (*laughing gently*). No. I can't see faces, how can I read numbers?

OTTO. Did Zauritz say anything at the time of the attack?

INGE. What?

OTTO. Did Zauritz say anything when he was attacked?

INGE. What's he going to say? I . . . I don't remember anything—

OTTO. Think, think, fires will rage if the newspaper can print his last words. Did Zauritz say anything when he was attacked?[33]

FOUR

At the court, the preliminary hearing is continuing in front of Justice Voss. On behalf of the police, Captain Hess is interrogating Dr Strubbel.

HESS. Dr Strubbel, did Zauritz say anything when he was attacked?

(*A very refined man, Strubbel is twirling an eye-catching snuff box on his fingers. On one side of the court are seated Lippert and Kurt. Landt and Otto too are present. Not too far away are radio announcers, news cameramen.*)

STRUBBEL. Look, I was inside the clinic. Through the open door, I could see, hazily, a group of people attacked Zauritz. With each blow of the knives, he groaned.

HESS. Who struck the first blow?

STRUBBEL. I told you that before.

---

33 In the video, the curtain opens behind them for the next scene.

voss. Tell us again.

STRUBBEL. The tall person slew first.

voss. Do you know anyone by the name of Richard Huettig?

STRUBBEL. No.

voss. Have you heard the name?

STRUBBEL. No. I have no enthusiasm for politics.

HESS. Then Zauritz could not say anything after receiving the blows?

STRUBBEL. I don't think so . . . wait, let me wear my glasses—(*wears his glasses*)—yes, I remember, wait—

HESS. You remember as soon as you wear your glasses?

STRUBBEL. Yes, these glasses are virtually my mind's glasses. My human eyes have got cataracts. When I put on my glasses, my inner vision opens.

(*Sounds of laughter.*)

voss. *Seien Sie still!*[34] A person's hanging trial may begin as a result of this investigation. I won't allow all this laughter in my court.

HESS. What did Zauritz say?

STRUBBEL. When the tall person stabbed him, he turned towards him and shouted, 'Why slay me?'

HESS (*disappointed*). Nothing more?

STRUBBEL. No. Then only shouts.

voss. Say what he said in his language. If needed, wear more powerful glasses and say it.

STRUBBEL. In his language?

voss. Yes, exactly as he said it.

---

34 'Remain quiet!'

STRUBBEL. That's what I said[35]—(*Shouting hideously*) '*Ach, warum schlachten Sie mich?*'—'What's this, why do you slay me?'

VOSS. There's no need to scream so much.

HESS. What did you do after the killers escaped?

STRUBBEL. I ran up to the body. Eleven blows. As a result of a blow on the neck, the head had virtually separated from the trunk. I've written all that in the report.

HESS. *Das ist alles*,[36] Herr General.

(*At a sign from Voss, Strubbel moves from the witness chair.*)

ANNOUNCER (*into the mike*). Berliner Rundfunk. On behalf of Berlin Radio Station, Hans[37] Taussig providing you a live account from the Berlin High Court of the preliminary hearing in the Zauritz murder case. Just now you heard Dr Strubbel's testimony. This morning you heard Mrs Zauritz's testimony. After hearing these two people's words, each one of you, except necessarily idiots, the ignorant or Soviet agents, will hold the Communist Party's local leader Richard Huettig and his associates responsible for this abominable homicide. Huettig will be brought to this room a little later, for identification and questioning.

(*On the other side, Hess continues speaking, but Voss cannot hear all that because of the radio commentator's screaming. Now he pounds the gavel*—)

---

35 In the video, he pauses here, raises his hands dramatically and shouts, shocking everyone in court.

36 'That is all.'

37 The Dramatis Personae names 'Anneliese' Taussig, enacted by a woman at the premiere, but in both texts the announcer introduces himself as Hans. In the video, the role returned to an actress, Bishnupriya Dutt, Dutt's daughter.

VOSS. What's all this?

TAUSSIG. *Rundfunkübertragung.*[38] It's a relay, Honourable Justice.

VOSS. Kapitan Hess, why is there all this trouble in the court? Who has given them the right to impede the work of the court?

HESS. The Chancellor himself, Herr General. Prime Minister Hitler himself.

VOSS. Why the Chancellor, even the President cannot violate the rights of the court. I'll see to this matter later. At present I caution radio and film employees—if you raise your voices, I'll throw you out of the court. Yes, what were you saying, say it.

HESS. After searching Huettig's hideout this knife was found, with dried blood on its handle and blade. And this coat was found, on it too the marks of blood are clear. Besides, after searching the Communist Party office, this bundle of handbills was found, it appears they had a plan to distribute this among the populace.

VOSS. Read it out.

(*Taussig comes and pushes the mike near Hess' face. In front of Voss' glare, she goes back again.*)

HESS (*glasses placed tightly, reads*). To the common people of Charlottenburg. 'Friends, the labourers' army has again rained blows on the enemy. Josef Zauritz used to reside in this area, and, unknown to you, used to work as a police detective, and regularly gave news to the police about the movements of labourers' leaders in this area. Last week this individual attacked the Communist Party through vile language expressed in a statement, casting off his mask of safety and liberalism. This agent has been given the ultimate punishment. Beware, all

---

38 'Radio broadcast.'

agents and spies! The Red Guards of the labourers' army are ready. —Ernst Telman[39], General Secretary, Communist Party of Germany.'

(*Commotion in the court; Taussig's voice rises somewhat.*)

LIPPERT. Herr General, this leaflet—

TAUSSIG. Did you hear? Did you? The handbill read out by Captain Hess just now on behalf of the police proves conclusively that—

VOSS. Quiet, quiet!

(*Bauer and Mueller come and lay their hands on Taussig. Taussig's voice lowers quickly.*)

VOSS. What was Herr Lippert saying?

LIPPERT. I was saying, we need to be cautious about this leaflet. Are the police convinced about its authenticity?

HESS (*momentarily angry*). How will I judge their authenticity? These were found in their party office, that's authentic. I don't know more than that.

VOSS. Where were all these printed?

HESS. There's no printer's name. Everyone knows they have several illegal presses.

LIPPERT. We shouldn't pay heed to this sort of leaflet unless we're absolutely certain. Because then it won't be a killer's trial any longer, it'll be transformed into a comprehensive blow against an entire political group. That'll be the grave of German democracy.

---

39 Ernst Thälmann (1886–1944), Stalinist chairman of the German Communist Party 1925–33, and twice its presidential candidate. His paramilitary Red Front was banned in 1929. The Gestapo arrested him in March 1933 in Charlottenburg. Hitler ordered him shot in Buchenwald in 1944.

LANDT (*to Otto, in a gentle tone*). People say about these Nazis, they're enemies of democracy!

VOSS. I assure Herr Lippert, nobody can entangle this court in political slaughter even if they try. Show me the leaflet. (*Runs his eyes over it*) Where's this Ernst Telman? Why isn't he being arrested?

HESS. He's gone into hiding, Herr General. Meanwhile three warrants hang against his name—all accusations of killing.

LIPPERT. I have something to say. The highest Communist Party leaders have all been compelled to go into hiding as a result of police harassment. You're a tough obstacle on the path to nationalism and socialism. The leader of the race, Adolf Hitler, wants to defeat the Communists forever through the medium of unobstructed, free elections. You're not letting him do it—you're compelling the Communists to build a secret organization.

(*Landt, Kurt, Bauer, Mueller applaud. Cameras start up with rattling sounds.*)

TAUSSIG. The thundering voice you heard just now—was that of the Nazi Party leader, Standartenfuehrer of the SS Unit, Johann Lippert. He is still standing. His golden hair shines as the light falls on—

VOSS. This is intolerable. This is a court. You think you're at a circus? (*Silence*) I've been judging for twenty years, I've never seen this kind of carnival taking over a court. There's no obstacle to accepting this leaflet as proof. We hope Huettig's lawyer will help ascertain its authenticity when the trial begins. Now let Richard Huettig be brought to court. Adjourned till then. Well, radio-wallah! Now you can scream as much as you please!

(*But the radio-wallah looks quite shamefaced. Voss drinks a cup of coffee, having come down from his high seat. He goes towards Lippert,*

Lippert stands up and proffers a salute, with a formidable click of his shoes.)

Herr Lippert, I'm very pleased after hearing your words. May your peaceful tone of voice be unbroken in the middle of the two extremist warring groups in bloody Germany today.

(At Landt's instigation, Otto comes near Voss.)

OTTO. Herr General, I come on behalf of the *Freie Zeitung* paper.

VOSS. You won't get an interview.

OTTO. No, no, not an interview, I only want to know what's your opinion about the hearing so far?

VOSS. A judge has no opinions, he sets himself afloat on the current of facts. One who wants to know the judge's opinion before the case begins is ignorant.

OTTO *(laughing gently)*. This you've said right, of course. One more question: Why does everybody call you General?

VOSS. Didn't I say you won't get an interview?

(Mueller and Bauer come and stand on either side of Otto. Otto is taken aback.)

What's all this? Is this Berlin or Chicago! He enters the court and interrogates the Justice. Although the rule's that the Justice does the interrogating. Besides, I know your face. Did you ever come to my court as a defendant?

OTTO. Never.

VOSS. I don't normally make mistakes. I have a feeling I jailed you for three months or so—probably on an accusation of swindling.

OTTO. No, no.

VOSS. Then perhaps I didn't, but I will. Don't sidle up to me.

(*Escaping, Otto comes near Landt, and at Landt's instigation proceeds toward Strubbel.*)

OTTO. Dr Strubbel, I come on behalf of the *Freie Zeitung* paper.

STRUBBEL. Wonderful. Won't you take pictures? Where's the camera?

(*Otto flourishes a camera.*)

Not from that side, from this. The left half of my face comes well. If you print this picture, your paper's prestige will increase.

OTTO. Now, Doctor, I have one or two questions.

STRUBBEL. Tell me.

OTTO. As far as you've heard and seen, what do you think?

STRUBBEL. What do I think about what?

OTTO. Meaning, is the Communist Party responsible for this killing? What do you say?

STRUBBEL. I don't say anything.

OTTO. Don't say anything? Intelligent people should have very clear opinions on all subjects.

STRUBBEL. You stay in Berlin, don't you? Or have you come visiting from London?

OTTO. In Berlin.

STRUBBEL. Residing in Berlin, how can you say intelligent people have opinions on all subjects? Just the opposite. All intelligent individuals in Berlin have resolved that the very concept of opinions is dangerous. Look, I'm probably the single individual on earth who reads the solemn books of Nietzsche and Marx with pleasure like novels. And I regard Nietzsche and Marx as pleasurably readable but unrealistic novels. In reality, I don't go anywhere asserting Nietzsche or Marx, since this is Berlin. Here I first have to see in which neighbourhood I'm standing. Suppose I go to Jerusalem Strasse and recite some delicate passage from Marx endowed with literary virtue, it would be grievous stupidity, because that's a Nazi locality, they can't tolerate Marx, they'd turn me into a martyr at once. On the other hand, if I go to the Wallstrasse locality and utter Nietzsche's verse I'll attain the same martyrdom again, because that's a Red locality and Nietzsche's poison in their eyes. You're writing all this, right?

OTTO. Yes, here, look—[40]

STRUBBEL. Yes, yes, write it down, you won't get such literature anywhere without paying. So you see, in Berlin, the concept of views is very much a secret matter, like venereal diseases. Since it's hard to keep track of which locality's been grabbed by whom and when. The single way to understand a neighbourhood's mood in this chaos is to read the writing on the walls. The neighbourhood on whose walls you'll see 'Kill the Communists to conclude killings', you'll understand is a Nazi one. And the one where you'll see 'Knock off the Nazis to conclude killings', you'll understand is a Red one. But the matter doesn't end there. There's no certainty that the locality grabbed by some today will remain under them tomorrow. Suppose you belch Marxist opinions ecstatically to humour boys in a Red neighbourhood today. Two days later, you'll see Nazi boys around you. Then that little opinion uttered at a weak moment will, with the logic of a bamboo stick, fly at your buttocks. Again, there are such localities where they won't even ask which novelist's devotee you are—just because you're a person from a different neighbourhood, all of them will thrash you to death suspecting you're a spy. Naturally, therefore, Berlin's intelligentsia has rejected the concept called

---

40 In the video, Otto shows his notebook, Strubbel says 'What's all this you've written?', Otto explains, 'Shorthand', and they laugh.

opinion. Keeping a hundred hands away from those two groups, I speak in the high-minded Shakespeare's language: 'A plague on both your houses.'[41] May both your families be seized by pestilence. You, too, won't reveal your views if you want to survive.

OTTO. I'll reveal them because I'm not intelligent, I'm ignorant. All right, how many years have you been in Wallstrasse?

STRUBBEL. Three years.

OTTO. That's a Red locality.

STRUBBEL. Diehard Red. Of course, now that Zauritz is dead, the police have entered and are ransacking the neighbourhood. The Nazis, too, after taking out processions for two days, have entered the neighbourhood.

OTTO. You're in that neighbourhood for three years, yet you don't know Huettig?

STRUBBEL. No, no, I'm not in all that. I met a middle-level Communist leader, his name's Zander. After we shook hands, I counted my fingers to see if all were there or he'd kept a couple. Thieving, cheap looks. Don't write this, for I have to return to the neighbourhood. I don't go out on the paths. When evening falls, I close the main door and drink, hear Beethoven's music on records and read books about boxing.

OTTO. A fellow named Meissner was killed there, on that subject—

STRUBBEL. No, I don't know anything on that subject. Zauritz knew, see what happened as a result? I won't ever know.

OTTO. All right, that Justice there, why does everybody call him General?

---

41 Mercutio in *Romeo and Juliet*, III.i: 'A plague a' both your houses!'

STRUBBEL. Because he was an army general. Now judging is his profession. He's Prussian, exceedingly belligerent and rough.

OTTO. All right, what's your view about the Nazi leader Lippert?

STRUBBEL. No view at all, no view at all. I'm nowhere near views. Don't I have to reside in Berlin?

(*Voss occupies his seat and pounds the gavel; everyone takes their respective seats.*)

VOSS. *Der Angeklagte*[42] Richard Huettig.

HESS. *Da ist er, mein* General.[43]

VOSS. *Lassen Sie ihn heraufrufen.*[44] The accused Richard Huettig should appear.

TAUSSIG. Now—now they're bringing in Richard Huettig. Richard Huettig, age 36, profession was steel labourer, presently whole-time worker of the Communist Party and Secretary of the Charlottenburg District Committee. Today's daily *Angriff* paper[45] writes in a title spanning the front page, 'Charlottenburg's terror Richard Huettig arrested'. In the past, the lives of Charlottenburg's inhabitants had become unendurable due to the tyranny of this individual, killing and rioting had become everyday incidents in that area.

(*Mueller and Bauer bring in the tall and burly Richard Huettig. His face bears signs of tremendous assault.*)

Richard Huettig enters the courtroom. His violent bestial face bears the signature of many bloody riots. On him a leather jacket, hair dishevelled—

---

42 'The accused.'

43 'He's there, my General.'

44 'Let's summon him.'

45 *Der Angriff*, a virulent Nazi mouthpiece. The Bengali texts misprint it as *Angrik*.

(*Film camera brought very near Huettig's face and taking pictures. Suddenly Voss bursts out—*)

VOSS. Captain Hess, I don't want to hear another word. The radio-wallahs and film-wallahs are all arrested. Arrested for contempt of court. Take them to the lockup. Immediately.

(*The room resounds with the tumult of begging pardon—*)

TAUSSIG. *Entschuldigen Sie bitte,* Herr Richter,[46] this will never happen again.

VOSS. Keep it in mind. Richard Huettig, what marks are on your face?

HUETTIG. Assault. For two days in the police station I've been hit regularly, in the mornings and evenings.

VOSS. Who hit you?

HUETTIG. Two inspectors taking turns—one's name is Dressler, the other's Homeier. The police station's Number 12 Charlottenburg Polizeiwache.

VOSS. Why are they hitting you in this manner?

HUETTIG. That I can't say, Herr Richter. They only say—Speak! Speak! I can't even understand what to speak.

VOSS. Captain Hess, why has the prisoner been assaulted in this manner? What's your explanation?

HESS. Herr General, I will take steps without delay.

VOSS. Those two inspectors must be present in my court tomorrow morning, otherwise you too will have to be accused of assault.

HESS. Both of them will be present, Herr General.

VOSS. I am stunned seeing your audacity. Until the offence has been proved, the defendants in my court are not guilty. Those

---

46 'Please excuse me, Herr Judge.'

who have laid hands on Richard Huettig will have to receive punishment. I hope that the Police Department will dismiss them both within 24 hours—otherwise I'll have your boss too, Police Commissioner Von Baden, stand here in the dock, keep it in mind.

HESS. *Jawohl,*[47] Herr General.

VOSS. Richard Huettig, did you on January 30 last, at two in the afternoon on the street of Wallstrasse, knife and murder Josef Zauritz?

HUETTIG. No.

VOSS. Where were you at that time?

HUETTIG. In Rudolf's liquor shop on Rosinenstrasse.

VOSS. Did anyone see you there?

HUETTIG. Yes, many. Rudolf, Heinz Preuss, Bruno, Franz Zander, Paul Schall—many of us were sitting and talking.

HESS. I have a question: They are all Communist Party members?

HUETTIG. Sure, they are. I'm the party's District Secretary. Will I chat with the Nazis?

VOSS. When the trial begins, will you call them as witnesses?

HUETTIG. Certainly.

HESS. They won't give false testimony to save their leader?

VOSS. I will judge whether the testimony's true or false. Continue questioning.

HESS (*picking up some books*). Herr Huettig, are these books yours?

HUETTIG (*looking*). Yes.

HESS. These books were found after searching his room, Justice.

VOSS. What books? Read their names.

---

47 Or *Ja*, 'Yes.'

HESS. Marx's *Kapital*, Engels' *The Peasant War in Germany*, Lenin's *The State and Revolution*.

VOSS. Captain Hess, are all these books illegal?

HESS. No, Herr General, but then—

VOSS. Then by what sense are you wasting the court's time? By what reasoning have you stolen and brought his books here?

HESS. Stolen! No, Justice, to make you understand the person's mentality I—

VOSS. The accused's mentality is not within your purview. Say what he has done or not done. It appears your wisdom and intelligence are not sufficient for more than that. Return the books to him—immediately.

HESS. *Jawohl*, Herr General. (*Deposits the books in Huettig's hands.*)

LIPPERT. If the charge of administration's in their hands, Shakespeare too will be banned soon.

VOSS. Continue questioning.

HESS. Herr Huettig, is this knife yours?

HUETTIG. No.

HESS. But this knife was found in your room.

HUETTIG. False. I've never seen this knife in my life.

VOSS. Are you saying the police have conspired to pass off this bloodstained knife as yours?

HUETTIG. Yes.

HESS. Herr Huettig, think well and say: This knife is not yours?

HUETTIG. No, not mine.

HESS. Can this knife be seen commonly in Berlin markets?

HUETTIG. That it can't, but anything invaluable doesn't mean it has to be mine.

HESS. It doesn't. All right, this mark that's on the handle—I mean, the colour's come off slightly—even seeing this you don't remember whether the knife's yours?

HUETTIG. Not I don't remember, but I do remember clearly the knife's not mine.

HESS. Now look at this photo—this too was found in your room. Will you say this picture too isn't yours? (*Huettig is startled.*) Of course, to say that is hard. Because you're in the picture yourself. And there's a woman. This picture is yours, right?

HUETTIG. Yes.

HESS. Justice, this was taken at least a year ago. Herr Huettig, I see in the picture, the two of you are sitting in some park, and you're opening a tin of meat with a knife. You see the knife in your hand? (*Huettig does not answer.*) The knife in the picture is shaped unerringly like this knife. Moreover, you see you can recognize clearly the discoloured mark on the handle. Did the police conspire to tuck a knife in your hand, lead you to the park, take and keep a picture of you a year ago so that they could frame you in this case by staining blood on that knife today?

(*Commotion in the court. Huettig is worried.*)

VOSS. Show me the picture.

HESS. Notice, Justice, the knife's shape is unusual—that knife's in the photo. Compare the two marks on the handles.

VOSS (*looks, then raises his eyes towards Huettig*). Richard Huettig, will you still say this knife isn't yours?

HUETTIG. I want the advice of my counsel. Without a lawyer, I won't reply to this question.

VOSS. That is your right. Get a lawyer at the time of trial. But understand one thing: if you don't answer questions at the preliminary hearing, you lose the court's confidence. (*Makes a sign to Hess.*)

HESS (*raising a bloodstained coat*). Is this coat yours?

HUETTIG. No.

HESS. You're unnecessarily harassing us. This coat is not yours?

HUETTIG. No.

HESS. Open your leather jacket. Wear this coat. Let's see whether it fits you or not.

(*Upon Huettig raising a questioning gaze, Voss says—*)[48]

VOSS. Of course you can legally decline to wear the coat, but I've already said the result will not be good.

HUETTIG. I won't wear the coat.

HESS.[49] That is, you virtually acknowledge that the coat is yours. And it has been proved that the knife is yours. Herr Huettig, you killed Zauritz.

HUETTIG. No.

HESS. Even if you say 'no' a thousand times, my impression is that the court has made up its mind on this subject, because you can't blow away a bloodstained knife and a bloodstained coat by saying 'no'. (*He sits.*)

VOSS. Call Frau Ingeborg Zauritz for the identification.

(*The court holds its breath—Ingeborg comes with slow footsteps.*)

---

48 In the video, Hess has thrown the coat into Huettig's lap while speaking. Huettig doesn't look up or at Voss, but takes the coat and drops it next to his chair.

49 The Complete Plays names Voss as the speaker. Obviously these lines belong to Hess, following the first edition.

VOSS. Frau Zauritz, I am ashamed to require your appearance here repeatedly—*Es tut mir sehr leid.*[50]

INGE. It's not an inconvenience for me.

VOSS. Frau Zauritz, do you know Richard Huettig?

INGE. Yes.

VOSS. Is he in this room?

INGE. Yes. Over there.

VOSS. All the proof that has been produced in front of this court up till now gives us enough cause to think that this blood-stained knife is Huettig's. Now you tell us: The tall person who first knifed your husband according to your statement, is he Richard Huettig?

INGE (*as soon as she places a hand on the knife, withdraws it*). Is this my husband's blood?

VOSS. There's enough cause to think as much.

INGE. Then you've got your proof. Why drag me into this again?

VOSS. The case becomes easy if you identify Huettig as the murderer.

(*Inge turns slowly towards Huettig.*)

INGE. How are you, Richard? What's this? So they hit you?

HUETTIG (*laughing*). A little, how are you, Frau Zauritz?

INGE. It'll probably take time to get used to widowhood.

HUETTIG. Frau Zauritz, I'm sorry that I can't do any more than convey ineffective sympathy on behalf of my party on your husband's death.

HESS. Justice, if you allow the two of them to talk in this manner—

VOSS (*rebuking*). Keep quiet.

---

50 'I am awfully sorry.'

INGE. And will you convey sympathy on my boy's death too, Richard?

HUETTIG. Boy's death?

INGE. It can be called a death. Paul was a boy full of tenderness and affection. The girl he loved, her name was Clara. In the evenings, the two of them would sit and read Heine's poems, my husband and I sat and listened. Richard, why did you snatch the boy away?

HUETTIG. Frau Zauritz, Paul's tenderness, affection, love have become vast and huge now, wanting to embrace the workmen on this planet. You call this death? Your breast should fill up with pride. This new love's strength builds barricades, causes the stormy winds of revolution to start flowing. Frau Zauritz, on behalf of the party I congratulate you for Paul.

INGE (*in a piercing voice*). I've heard Ludwig Meissner's shouts with my own ears. My boy Paul Schall has metamorphosed into a killer cannibal, he hasn't a drop of love anywhere in his breast for anyone, all dried up. Only his eyes, owing to old habits, seem to occasionally search for someone. Probably for his mother, but can't find her. Why did you drag him into the primitive jungle? You'll fight the elections, snatching and killing for the cushions—but what will happen to Paul? For he has dipped his hands in blood and become a fugitive, what'll happen to him? His mind's frozen into ice, who'll melt it? He feels happy when he kills, where's the remedy for this terrible injustice? Richard, how many boys like this have you destroyed? How many boys have you abducted from mothers' laps and turned into goons, how many have you made prey for the police?

HUETTIG (*loudly*). Frau Zauritz! We're fighting with our backs to the wall, to save our lives. Open your eyes to see: Who's slaying whom? The country's becoming red with Communists' blood. That's why we've been compelled to take up weapons.

INGE. Old Josef Zauritz, aged 70, went to slay you?

HUETTIG. We didn't slay him. Listen, Frau Zauritz—

INGE (*shouting*). No, I won't listen any more. Now I'll speak. Reply— Whose knife is this? Whose blood? What history is written here in dried blood? You'll destroy many other mothers, take the lives of many other boys, push many others onto the gallows. I won't let that happen. Paul may have gone, I'll have to save the other Pauls. Honourable Justice, although my eyes are bad, still, as far as I can tell, this Richard Huettig is that tall person who first knifed my husband. (*Commotion in court*) Nourished by my husband's affection and indulgence this ungrateful, unfaithful Huettig killed him with a knife!

(*A wan smile blooms on Huettig's face.*)

VOSS. Richard Huettig, the preliminary accusation against you is proven. You are committed to sessions. Your trial will begin next week. The accusation against you—last January 30, at two in the afternoon on the street of Wallstrasse, you murdered Josef Zauritz with a knife.

(*A tumult begins on radio and film in one body.*)

TAUSSIG. Did you hear? Did you hear? The Communist killer Richard Huettig will be tried. His offence has been proved at the preliminary hearing. The real nature of the Communists' politics of murder has been uncovered in front of the world.

(*Amidst tremendous tumult, the front page of the* Freie Zeitung *in massive form comes down from above. On it, the enormous headline: 'The Communists did the killing'.*[51] *The newspaper is partly*

---

51 The intermission should occur here. In the video, nothing flies down, but all the characters on stage turn to hear Taussig and freeze in a

transparent. From inside it can be seen Adolf Hitler speechifying in front of a row of mikes, with his famous or infamous power. And in front can be gradually seen Landt, listening to that speech on the radio and occasionally working.)

FIVE[52]

HITLER. The Communists' real nature has been uncovered—they're not men, they're beasts—otherwise they wouldn't have brutally murdered the old patriot Zauritz. They're not Germans, their bodies have black Asian blood. They're a poisonous sore on this country's health. They're the hired agents of Moscow's Jewish intrigue. Look at their ensign—that hammer and sickle they've borrowed from Russia. It's not our ensign, there's no place in nationalistic Germany for them. They're enemies of democracy, obstacles to socialism. Go to election centres on 5 March with the name of Zauritz, old leader of the race, on your lips, by the strength of votes uproot the Asiatic disease named egalitarianism from this country.

(Meanwhile Otto has come, on his head a feather-topped Tyrol hat, a sheaf of papers in his hand. Hearing the awesome roar on the radio, he stops, startled. Seeing him, Landt lowers the radio volume. Hitler's picture fades away but his voice continues playing on the airwaves.)

LANDT. Come, Otto.

OTTO. You called me?

---

tableau. From this point on, the rest of this stage direction applies to Scene Five. See the next note.

52 Neither printed text demarcates this as Scene Five, but both number Scene Six in its proper place later.

LANDT. Yes. Sit, a few words with you. (*Lifts the phone*) Get me Grossman. (*To Otto*) What have you started? At one time you used to write forcefully— (*On the phone*) Grossman? What's this you've written? . . . I'm talking of the report on the police firing at Magdeburg . . . listen to what I'm saying, you're screaming continuously. I'm not saying the report's false. I'm talking of your odd language. You've written (*reads*) 'Then the police fired and three labourers in the procession died of it.' What is this? Have you been drinking or what? . . . Can't you understand? First, such words as 'the police fired' cannot come out in my paper. You'll write, 'the police were compelled to fire.' . . . I don't want to hear arguments. The police are always compelled. They can't fire—don't fire unless they're compelled. That's the rule. Second, when they have to be compelled, where's the cause for compelling them? . . . I know very well the labourers took out a procession for the Magde-burg strike, but that can't be written—you can't just leave it after writing that. You don't understand anything about journalism. The labourers take out a procession like a herd of harmless sheep and the police launch a raid, you can't print these words. The police can't be compelled by strikers taking out a procession. Therefore I'm writing the thing in this manner—'When the police went to search the terrorist Communists' den, they rained bullets on the police. As a result the police were compelled to shoot in retaliation.' (*Otto was leaving*) Where are you going? Sit. (*On the phone*) No, I know you're sitting. I said that to Otto. Third, you've written 'three labourers died'. What is this? . . . No, no, all that won't do. Whoever dies of police bullets, he's always an armed terrorist. The police don't slay anyone else, at least not in the news-papers. Therefore I'm altering it to write, 'Two terrorists died, one was slain by their own bullets.'[53] Fourth, I'm adding after this, 'From the hideout four Russian rifles, ten pistols, plenty of cartridges, Lenin's books and some manifestos were found.' Now it's clear why the police were compelled. In my paper it'll be like this. If you don't like it hand in your resignation. (*Puts down the phone*) Otto, are you having trouble with your digestion?

OTTO. Why do you say that?

LANDT. Where's the energy in your writing? The flame? The whole of Germany is in turmoil over the Zauritz murder case, and each and every one of your reports assumes the form of such tasteless watery bitter that I have to stay awake the whole night putting crushed chillies and other spices into it. What is this? This weird hat?[54] Now I understand, your head's rotting inside. Why've you bought this hideous hat? Don't people laugh?

OTTO. Sure they laugh. They laugh and say, Look what an ugly hat!

LANDT. Then why wear it?

OTTO. Otherwise they all say, Look what an ugly person. This hat's a way to direct their sight on a different path. Besides it's convenient for my work if people laugh a lot. Laughing opens their mouths, they readily give statements. Only in front of you I see it hasn't done the trick.

LANDT. No, it won't do the trick, what's all this you're writing? The case is virtually over, everyone knows that Huettig's the killer—only you I see, very circumspectly, playing catch-fish-don't-touch-water. Well, what's the matter?

---

53 At this point in the video, Otto quickly grabs a liquor bottle from Landt's desk and takes a swig.

54 In the video, Otto ad libs, 'Yes, they gave it to me.' He wears a truly incongruous, pink, lady's hat. Perhaps he referred to the costume crew!

OTTO. Why, I report everything. I write whatever anyone says, to the letter—

LANDT. For that I could have kept a clerk. Like a strainer, a reporter lifts just the cream and puts it on the reader's plate—

OTTO. With crushed chillies, spices, flame—

LANDT. Mixing sugar, beating eggs, making pudding—it's now resounding over Germany's skies and winds that the Communists are the killers. Only in my paper I see stenographic reports being preserved of the conversations in court. You're giving vegetarian fare to the readers.

OTTO. You're not being inconvenienced by it. Reading the kind of headlines you release makes one's hair stand on end.

LANDT. But the stories don't match with the headlines. (*Slapping the table with tremendous speed; Otto is startled*) It's as if you see a beauty's face, go to kiss her, then see a hump on her back. Just a little while ago the telephone rang, I got scolded so much— to stop it.

OTTO. Who scolded you?

LANDT. Some higher-up!

OTTO. Since he can scold you, must be the highest government body. Who's he?

LANDT. You don't have to know the name. In short, why do you write saving the Communists, give me a reply.

OTTO (*drinking liquor*). Because this case isn't so easy. The more I enter inside, the more I see that people aren't what I thought them to be. He whom I thought straight is crooked. He whom I thought crooked—

LANDT. Is straight. Oof! Look Otto, don't try too much high thinking. In your hands, philosophy takes the shape of elfin rhymes. Your—

OTTO (*forcefully*). Why don't you hear my words. I can't be certain on this subject, that the Communists did the killing.

(*In tremendous amazement Landt stands up.*)

LANDT. Otto, have you secretly become a Communist Party member or what?

OTTO. Herr Landt, since when did you change so much?

LANDT (*perplexed*). Meaning?

OTTO. If I want to test the truth, you call me a Communist Party person. I'll have suspicions even if the whole earth screams as one. They'll have to be refuted.

LANDT (*composed again*). You have suspicions because of low intelligence. Can you deny that the knife is Huettig's? Isn't the bloodstained coat Huettig's? In the end, police chief Hess proved the coat is Huettig's in court with a tape measuring Huettig's chest, back and arms.[55] On top of that, there's an ugly, conscience-less plea for murdering humans in the Communist Party's leaflet.

OTTO. Listen, these are all very fearful matters. But I too have a few small causes for suspicion—(*about to drink liquor*)

(*At which point Hitler releases a tremendous bellow on the radio.*)

HITLER. What do those Communists want? (*Otto chokes, coughs away.*) I've given them democratic rights unobstructed, full rights to elections. But if such heinous homicides still continue repeatedly, let me utter a cautionary message—our patience has limits too.

(*Otto was tightening the cap on the bottle—upon the last bellow, the bottle falls from his hand.*)

---

55 In the video, Landt enacts this on Otto's back, Otto giggles, Landt says 'What happened?' and Otto replies, 'You're tickling me.'

OTTO. Shut it, sir, shut it. (*Landt shuts the radio.*) Oof! Nothing more remains of my eardrums. Everything about leaders is excessive. He's giving a speech ten miles away, and here life's becoming unendurable. (*Wiping the table and his outfit with a hanky*) Yes, I was saying—I have causes for suspicion.

LANDT. *Keineswegs!*[56] There aren't any causes.

OTTO. Ah, there are, I tell you, take the deposition of Zauritz's wife. She says the killers were screaming 'Long live the Communist Party'. If the Communists wanted to kill, why would they scream like that, why undo themselves by screaming?

LANDT. Communists are like that! You have a lamentable lack of common sense. Marx and Engels have said Communists detest keeping views secret. They're prepared to let the whole of Germany know by printing leaflets, and they can't scream at the time of killing? Read the *Communist Manifesto* by Marx and Engels some time, all will become plain.

OTTO. Then why's Huettig saying in court that he didn't kill? On one hand, they want to let everyone know they've slain. On the other, they say they haven't. Haven't they read the *Communist Manifesto* either?

LANDT. As an individual, Huettig feels afraid. Standing in the awful shadow of the gallows, many revolutionaries find their revolution-illness dispelled. But it's been truly proved that the party's firmly resolute and bloodthirsty.

OTTO. Again, that elderly lady says, they escaped in a car. Why? Wallstrasse is a Red locality, why a car? More surprisingly, the one who was driving asked the others, '*Wo muss ich einbiegen, Kamerad?*' Where's the corner? Which way do I turn, comrade? Really odd words. Huettig and company are people of that

---

56 'By no means!'

neighbourhood, yet one of them doesn't know the corners in the neighbourhood?

LANDT (*impatient*). My firm impression is that you tame flies.

OTTO. Sir?

LANDT. That day I saw you feeding, clothing and putting to sleep four flies upon the table.

OTTO. No, no, when did you see this?

LANDT. Unless one tames flies, one can't have such lowly sight. The whole country's overwhelmed, and you're taken up with this question of why the driver doesn't know the corners. This tunnel vision is learnt from flies. No other society has it.

OTTO. Still, I have to get a reply to this question. I have to go to the scene of the crime. I'm going to Wallstrasse—

LANDT. The Communists are there, they'll slay you.

OTTO. I have to see the scene of the crime, I have to ask the inhabitants there—

LANDT. Whose clutches have you fallen into, tell me? Whose money have you gobbled? Who's behind you? Which patron's force?[57] Who's caught you by the ears, making you stand up and sit down?

OTTO. Why drag my wife into this?

LANDT. Wife?

OTTO. Only my wife makes me stand up and sit down, no one else can. The way she catches my ears—that wife. No one else will have such courage as to touch my ears. I'm leaving then, going to Wallstrasse—

---

57 To each of these questions, Otto issues polite verbal denials in the video.

LANDT (*slapping the table*). No, you don't have to go. You're not a police person, you don't have to solve a newspaper mystery.

OTTO. If I don't solve the mystery how do I write? Let me know the truth before—

LANDT. *Teufel!*[58] I don't need truth, I want news. What I say you'll write.

(*Silence*)

OTTO. But that's not written on the back of your watch, Herr Landt, I don't need truth, I want news—these words aren't there. Why such a big divide between truth and news anyway?

LANDT (*head lowered*). I can't tell you everything. Because you don't know everything I can in this manner—a lot of water's flowed down the Rhine River. Many knots, many nooses have got into the string. Heinrich Landt's voice has broken, notes aren't coming out, the thundering tone's no longer thrown up by that voice!

OTTO. Why are you in this condition? From drinking cold beer?

LANDT. Go, remove yourself. Go to Wallstrasse. And look—do die from the Communists' bombs there, our readers will heave a sigh of relief.

OTTO. That won't happen. The wife's forbidden me to die.

SIX

Wallstrasse—at the Rosinenstrasse crossing, in Rudolf's liquor shop, Rudolf was behind the counter and Franz Zander, sitting at a table, was writing on a slip of paper. Beside him, Willi standing. And everywhere Nazis' posters—'Communist dogs beware!' 'We want Huettig hanged' 'Hitler is leader of the race!' 'Vote for the Nazis!' etcetera.

---

58 'Devil!'

RUDOLF. Franz, heard the news?

ZANDER. Which one?

RUDOLF. Last night, the Nazis dragged out the small boy on the first floor and took him away. The fellow's name is Fritz. They took him to their haunt and hit him, the whole night. How the boy shouted! I don't think anyone in the neighbourhood could sleep.

ZANDER.[59] Hm? (*Giving the slip of paper to Willi*) Hand this over to Gottfried.

(*Willi goes, running.*)

RUDOLF. What do you think? From which side will they attack today?

ZANDER. How can I tell? They don't do things after discussing with me.

(*Bruno's excited entrance.*)

BRUNO. Rudolf, give me brandy real quick. (*After drinking brandy*) Oof, a terrible battle's about to happen. A tremendous battle. Understand, Franz, a battle's about to happen. (*On the telephone*) Hello Fraulein, get me Wilhelm 38–42.

RUDOLF. Who're you phoning?

BRUNO. The doctor. (*On the phone*) Doctor Himmelstoss? Bruno speaking. Be ready, perhaps I'll be coming to your clinic for treatment after a little while . . . no, I'm not injured yet, however a terrible battle's about to happen, I may be injured. (*Puts the phone down.*)

RUDOLF. Where's the battle?

---

59 The Complete Plays names Rudolf as the speaker. Obviously these lines belong to Zander, following the first edition.

BRUNO. Here.

RUDOLF. What's that? With whom?

BRUNO. You with me. I can't pay for the brandy.[60]

(*Zander laughs out. Rudolf picks up a bottle to throw—*)

RUDOLF. *Schweinhund!*[61] (*Bruno escapes, coming near Zander.*) This Bruno should be tossed in jail. He never pays. He'll empty the shop, swilling away without spending.

BRUNO. I don't have money, you bloodsucking skinflint petit bourgeois. So I have to toil my intelligence to lead a life in this society somehow, to eat by cheating you. Well Franz, why do you come to this neighbourhood in this manner, all alone? You fancy becoming a martyr?

ZANDER. There's a guard outside. Sit.

BRUNO. What's the need? Why call me?

ZANDER. You have to go to Koepenick. To this address—

BRUNO. What's the matter?

ZANDER. They'll give you election leaflets.

BRUNO. No, no, I'm no longer into childishness. I'm no longer into elections!

ZANDER. The party will decide where you'll be or won't be. Or are you determining everything yourself these days?

BRUNO. I ought to. My impression's that all the leaders have grown fat by overeating. If we're in their hands we'll all die. They're fighting the elections with the Nazis. Alas, ignoramus, you still don't know about bourgeois elections?

---

60 In the video, Rudolf says 'Okay' genially, then does a double-take.
61 Abuse, literally 'Swine-dog!'

ZANDER. You're talking too much these days. That's dangerous! You'll get caught.

BRUNO. Your impression's we will win the elections?

ZANDER. Certainly. There's no point shouting about the Zauritz murder. All people also understand there's no point in the Nazi goons conducting raids. Their own violent faces get exposed. We'll win the elections.

BRUNO. *Dummkopf!*[62] Ignorant. What faith in the bourgeois! They'll let you win the election? And even if you win, they'll let you run the government? You've seen it for five years, still you don't get wise. The bourgeois will hug you, feed you sausages, seat you on the cushion, doff their hats, salute you, suppress the sorrows in their minds and go where their eyes lead them. With such deep respect for bourgeois righteousness and magnanimity, how are you in the Communist Party? Your place is in the Nazi Party, I see.

ZANDER (*laughing*). These words have been exchanged many times, Bruno, why are you annoying me? Do you see me escape at the time of fighting?

BRUNO (*in gentle tones*). No, of course not. Instead you advance in such a way, you bastard, it isn't right. Such a desire to meet one's maker can't be seen commonly. You have a disposition for suicide.

ZANDER. I'll fight with a gun finally, but why should I leave the fight by votes! You'll go to Koepenick in the afternoon. Tell this person: Can you show me which way's the church? Then he'll—

BRUNO. No, no, all those passwords are fruitless.

ZANDER. That is?

---

62 'Blockhead!'

BRUNO. Your impression is a secret organization is built by saying all that. Bastard, you electoral revolutionaries know nothing about secret organizations. Last week you sent me to Karl-shorst[63]—a comrade named Kruegel apparently lives there, I have to go to him and say a secret, very secret password: 'Where do I get milk here?' You know what an affair it was? I matched the house's number and knocked at the door. A bald person opened. I asked: You're Kruegel, aren't you? He said yes. I bent just a little and started the very secretive, sacred password: Where do I get—. That's it! He didn't let me say more. Screaming, he said: You're searching for Kruegel the Communist, aren't you? He lives on the first floor. I'm Kruegel the barber. Saying which he banged the door shut. There's your secret organization, you bastard. It's disgusting. (*Stuffs the slip of paper in his pocket*) I'll return in the evening. How many leaflets will he give?

ZANDER. Twenty thousand.

BRUNO. Okay.

(*Paul brings Otto in. Otto is literally taken aback.*)

PAUL. This gentleman wants to meet Franz Zander.

ZANDER. I'm Zander. Sit down. What do you need?

OTTO. *Guten morgen.*[64] I'm Otto Birkholz, a reporter for the *Freie Zeitung* paper.

ZANDER. *Freie Zeitung*! (*Takes out that day's paper.*) I see that even before the trial's over you've labelled us 'killers', now what more do you want?

OTTO. No, no, that's the headline. Read the story, you'll see it's written in a completely different temperament.

---

63 A suburb of Berlin. Wrongly transliterated as 'Karlsist' in the Bengali.
64 'Good morning.'

ZANDER (*throwing the paper on the table*). Forgive me, I have neither time nor inclination to read this kind of slander. What do you want? This area's converted into a war zone now twice daily, what necessity do you have here?

OTTO. I want an interview. I have some questions.

ZANDER. You won't print our replies, so what's the use of questioning?

OTTO. We will print, certainly we'll print. Listen, what's your view about Huettig's trial?

ZANDER. What view? The case is false from start to finish. Our party's being tangled in a false case.

OTTO. With what objective?

ZANDER. To defeat us in the elections. And, second, facilitate the path for police and goons to enter this area on the pretext of the Zauritz murder. If you go outside you'll see a group of hoodlums camping on Wallstrasse under the police's strict guard. Over these few days they've caught and thrashed fifteen of our members, arrested thirty-nine. They want to uproot us from this neighbourhood.

OTTO. You feel they'll be able to uproot you?

ZANDER. It's not possible to throw a bomb inside a man's mind, so they won't be able to do that in their lives. Let them remove the police, the machineguns, for a few hours, see what we do.

BRUNO. The only problem then will be where we'll bury the Nazi hoodlums. Because, as you can see, this locality's slightly congested, there's a slight lack of empty space. (*Bruno presents himself again at Rudolf's durbar.*)

OTTO. All right, Richard Huettig's case—

ZANDER. Look, I've got work. (*To Bruno*) *Genosse!*

BRUNO. *Ja?*

ZANDER. Reply to his questions.

OTTO. What did you call him?

ZANDER. *Genosse*, comrade.

OTTO. Oh.

BRUNO (*to Rudolf*). You ought to give two brandies, at least, for hospitality's sake.

RUDOLF. No way, go.

BRUNO. Then give me an empty glass and half a lemon.

RUDOLF. What for?

BRUNO. To drink. Or will you want the lemon's price? Will you want rent for the glass? What with your atrocious mentality.[65] (*With lemon and glass, Bruno comes near Otto*) If you require beer or whatever, buy it. We don't have money. (*Squeezes lemon juice into the glass.*)

PAUL. What's going on?

BRUNO. I'll drink a glass full of lemon juice.

PAUL. Have you lost your head? Where will you get a glass full of juice from such a tiny lemon?

BRUNO. I will, I will, when I squeeze it. If the government can squeeze us to still draw tax, then I'll be able to fill a glass by squeezing this lemon.

(*Everyone laughs.*)

PAUL (*to Otto*). His name's Bruno. He was first a railway labourer, then a professional goon, then a professional boxer, then a vagrant, then a farmer, now a party worker.

---

65 In the video, Bruno calls Rudolf 'Frog in a well' and 'Petit bourgeois' repeatedly.

BRUNO. I don't like one job for too long. What do you want to know? I know everything.

OTTO. What's your people's assessment about the Huettig case?

BRUNO. Take this, our booklet. You'll find all in it. If you give me its price, that'll be very good, meaning the party's financial situation being—

PAUL. This booklet has sold 14 lakh copies till today.[66]

OTTO. All right, Herr Zander just said that Nazi goons and the police together are attacking you, but the Nazi leader Lippert denies this.

BRUNO. The Nazi leader Lippert also denies his own father, since Lippert's illegitimate. He doesn't even know who his father is. He can't quite understand whom to acknowledge.

PAUL. What's happening? Franz, he's messing up.

ZANDER. Let him speak! Nothing will be printed in that paper, therefore let him speak what he pleases.

BRUNO. Last year, in the month of December, Lippert shot to death with his own hands our party member, Walter Lange, a youth aged 24. The boy was lying face down on the road after a severe assault by Nazi goons. Then Lippert shot him through the back of his head. But what did he do after shooting him? In a swift action he brought out a hanky and wiped the pistol's handle. Can you say why?

OTTO. So that fingerprints don't remain?

BRUNO. *Das ist wahr.*[67] What's proved by this? It's proved that Lippert was a bandit before, wiping fingerprints after a kill had become a habit with him.

---

66 In the video, Otto takes money out and pays Bruno.

67 'That is correct.'

(*Laughter*)

PAUL. Rubbish. He was an economics professor before. *Genosse* Zander, this individual's making all kinds of harmful statements.

ZANDER. Let him, let him. With a paper like that, they are appropriate statements for it.

OTTO. You're repeatedly abusing my very dear *Freie Zeitung*, I won't tolerate it.

(*The Communists actually feel pleased at his firmness.*)

BRUNO. Have you kept any means for not abusing it? As soon as Zauritz was killed, even before any investigation began, let alone the trial, you laid the blame on the Communist Party's shoulders, meaning scapulae—why, meaning for what raison?[68]

PAUL. Why are you making the language so heavy?

BRUNO. I'm giving a statement. My impression's that your editor Landt is illegitimate too.

(*Otto starts, the pencil falls down from his hand. Meanwhile at Zander's sign Rudolf has brought a glass of beer for Otto.*)

BRUNO. Give, give it this side.

RUDOLF. Not for you, for the guest.

BRUNO. See? Our party's as hospitable as it's miserly.

OTTO. All right, till today how many members of your party have been killed?

BRUNO. *Ich weiss nicht.*[69] I don't keep that calculation.

PAUL. One and a half thousand.

---

68 Bruno starts speaking in formal Bengali for the record, sometimes falling back instinctively to colloquial language and correcting himself.
69 'I don't know.'

BRUNO. I only calculate how many I slay. How many of their illegitimates died, that's my day-and-night count. That is, how many Nazi illegitimates expired, is—

OTTO. How many arrested?

PAUL. Over five thousand.

OTTO. Aren't they tried?

(*Bruno and Paul laugh out.*)

BRUNO. If caught under the Security Act, they're not tried. After two years of toil in jail—meaning enjoying the pangs of incarceration—I arrived. I was a farmer then. My better half alone, by what procedure would she till the land?—Why aren't you writing all this?

OTTO. I am, I am, speak.

BRUNO. I do speak, I wrote to my wife then from jail, do not you till the land; you don't know I have kept some things buried in that place. Notice the word 'things'. Naturally the jail officer read that letter. Seven days later I got my bride's epistle: A terrible affair, two lorries of police did arrive, did dig up the entire land, attempting to locate concealed weapons; whatever should I do? Wherever should I go? In answer to it I wrote: Ignorant lass, wherever shall you go? Do sow seeds right now in that ploughèd land!

(*Everyone laughs.*)

OTTO. Oh, I understand, they tilled the land for you. Understood.

BRUNO. You have got acute intelligence.

OTTO. All right, are there beatings in jail?

(*Everyone laughs.*)

BRUNO. No, no, they bathe you in milk mixèd with butter.

PAUL. You get hit in three phases. First the Nazi Stormtroopers, then the police at the station. Then the warders in jail.

OTTO. What's this you're saying? Doesn't the country have laws, don't prisoners have rights?

(*Laughter again*)

BRUNO. Tell me, where do you live? A citizen of Berlin, aren't you?

OTTO. Doctor Strubbel asked me this question too. Hearing the question repeatedly my impression is, I . . . I'm lamentably detached from life. Apart from my wife and editor Landt, I don't know anyone. I'm enjoying the pangs of incarceration, you haven't. (*Pours some beer into Bruno's glass.*)

BRUNO. *Danke schoen.*[70]

RUDOLF. Don't give him any. The more he drinks, the more his thirst increases.

OTTO. They truly hit? You're not falsely propagating this? I know some of the methods of Communist propaganda.

ZANDER (*calling*). Heinz!

PAUL. You'll accept live proof?

(*Heinz Preuss comes walking with great difficulty, legs apart, file in hand. One hand dangles, disabled. Scars on the face, too.*)

HEINZ. There's a little left, Franz, if I write another half-hour—

ZANDER. Not for that! Come. (*Takes him near Otto.*) This is Heinz Preuss, age nineteen, got caught while writing on walls. Tell us, Heinz—

HEINZ. No, let all that be, there's work.

ZANDER (*in a firm tone*). Tell us.

---

70 'Thank you.'

HEINZ. They took me to the station, interrogated me, punched me in the face, pressed burning cigarettes here. Then they took me to the police head office in Charlottenburg. There Captain Hess himself laid me face down and shoved a fat iron rod into my anus—repeatedly. Then four of them jointly lifted and threw me against the wall. This continued for three days and three nights.

ZANDER. He won't be able to walk anymore in this life! They slew a boy named Klarfet by giving him electric shocks. (*Zander's hand unconsciously touches Heinz's head and plays with his hair.*)

OTTO. Has your health broken down totally?

HEINZ. So what if it has? My right hand is okay. I don't feel any inconvenience pressing a pistol's trigger.

OTTO. A civilized country—such hellish incidents occurring in this Berlin, pilgrimage centre of knowledge, science, wisdom?

BRUNO. In this Berlin, pilgrimage centre of wisdom, the police kill a journalist and poet like Erich Muehsam,[71] yet the wise don't make the feeblest sound.

OTTO. Who? Whose name did you say?

BRUNO. The poet Erich Muehsam. He was an anarchist. Once he was the coeditor of the *Berliner Zeitung* paper, your colleague. Haven't heard the name?

OTTO. Sure I have, I know him too. I haven't heard he's been killed.

BRUNO. The police arrested him in the evening. The next day at dawn his body was found inside Tiergarten park. There are eyewitnesses to this killing, Herr Birkholz.

---

71 The real Erich Mühsam (1878–1934), arrested on 28 February 1933, died the next year from vicious beatings and torture in a concentration camp. An anarchist writer and political activist, he attacked Nazism and satirized Hitler in his works. Dutt anachronistically connects him to the *Berliner Zeitung*, which began publication in 1945.

OTTO. But this news hasn't been published anywhere.

PAUL. Where's the time for it? Radio, press, government, police, Nazi Party are all only busy beheading the Communist Party.[72]

ZANDER. The attack's coming—Roentgenstrasse.

(*In one body the Communists bring out pistols and see whether bullets are loaded.*)

Bruno, give the news to the Red Guards. Paul, you're not going.

PAUL. Why?

ZANDER. They're searching for you. A wanted notice has come out in your name for the Zauritz murder case. Scram—to the Number 3 hideout.

BRUNO. Come bastards, I'll bury all of you today. Herr Birkholz, will you come? Come and see machineguns on the front and back of the police cars, and see the democratic expedition of the Nationalist Socialists in the middle?

OTTO. My wife's forbidden me to die.

BRUNO. Then come, we'll reach you to the corner.

OTTO. No, I've thought it out, I need to see all this—whatever the wife may say.

BRUNO. *Vorwärts Genossen, wir schützen die rote Fahne.*[73] This is the red flag's fight, remember that.

---

72 In the video, Willi runs in with a note that he hands to Zander.

73 'Forward, comrades, we'll protect the red flag.'

SEVEN

Justice Voss' chamber, Helga shows the way, bringing in Inge, Landt, Hess and Strubbel.

HELGA. You can sit here, Justice Voss will be coming. Doctor Strubbel, you're absolutely wet.

STRUBBEL. Yes, I lost my umbrella.

HELGA. When?

STRUBBEL. Just now. I was coming along fine. I entered this house, was going to close my umbrella, and saw it wasn't there—I was only holding my hand like this.

HELGA. Sit near the fire.

LANDT. Why did the Justice suddenly call for us; you know?

HELGA. Even if I did, I don't have orders to talk.

(*Helga exits. Everyone sits.*)

LANDT. Captain Hess, do you know?

HESS. No.

LANDT. I have misgivings.

HESS. What misgivings?

LANDT. No, look—the case is virtually over, Huettig has one foot on the gallows. There can be just one reason to suddenly call for us at this time, some new crisis has developed.

STRUBBEL. So why should you have misgivings?

LANDT. I mean, I've already said as much in my paper: Huettig's the offender. Now if, again—

STRUBBEL. That is, to keep your honour now Huettig ought to hang.

INGE.[74] Herr Landt, do you have today's paper?

LANDT. Yes.

INGE. Bring it out. Read out the headline.

LANDT. 'Communist prisoners rebel in jails. 311 dead after prison guards shoot.'

INGE. In one day 311 died inside jails?

LANDT. Yes.

INGE. In your view they had rebelled?

LANDT. Yes.

INGE. With what?

LANDT. It's written here: rope ladders, bombs and pistols were found on them. They were trying to escape. Haven't you read the paper?

INGE. I have. Since reading I feel a pain-like sensation in my mind—how did all those things reach the prisoners?

LANDT (*perplexed*). That I don't know.

INGE. This isn't the first. Counting this, there have been eight shootings in jails! Each time they try to escape with ladders, each time the prison guards fire—

LANDT. Are compelled to fire—

INGE. Yes, compelled to, and the unarmed prisoners in a completely helpless position run about within four walls and die. You don't call this barbarism?

LANDT. No doubt the matter's heinous. But violence has to be vanquished by violence. The Communists don't understand any

---

74 The Complete Plays gives this line to Strubbel. Following the first edition and video, I have given it to Inge.

other language. I hope this fact doesn't have to be explained to Josef Zauritz's wife.

STRUBBEL. Yes, the Communists are being slain, Frau Zauritz, therefore what's it to us? We're the highly civilized German race, consequently come let's read Goethe's poetry.

INGE (*with a wan smile*). I used to say that too, the Communists are being slain, what's it to us? Then, a few days ago I got to know that a warrant's been issued in the name of Paul, my boy. He's Communist, but how can his mother say any more, What's it to me? He'll go to jail too, and if they slay him you'll write: He tried to escape, so the prison guards were compelled to fire. I never thought I'd get entangled in the matter suddenly like this.

HESS (*while writing something*). Frau Zauritz, you know where Herr Paul Schall is? He can't be found.

INGE. You're even hoping this, Captain Hess, that I'll hand the boy over to you.

HESS. No, no, forgive me. I ought not to have said it like that.

INGE. Why ought not? Ask this Landt-sahib[75]. He'll say: Paul Schall's just a Communist, why should his mother object to handing him over?

LANDT. You're looking at the thing through personal emotion. Look at the matter keeping in mind the interests of race and country, those Communists are at the root of all of Germany's adversities.

INGE. Therefore Germany will dispel adversities by murdering untried prisoners, and take the best seat in the global

---

75 Dutt puns on the Bengali term *lāt sāheb*, derived from 'Lord', usually addressed to colonial officers.

community. (*Laughs*) If we abandon all humanity, what will Germany have left?

LANDT. Not all humanity, Communist violence has been abandoned. What will Germany have? Democracy, independence, peaceful life for citizens, citizens' rights in full.

INGE. Captain Hess.

(*Hess is writing something single-mindedly, does not reply.*)

STRUBBEL. Probably writing a letter to his wife. He writes all the time.

INGE. Why is he writing so slowly?

STRUBBEL. His wife can't read fast. So he writes slowly. Really loves his wife. Captain Hess!

HESS (*reverie broken*). *Ich bitte um Entschuldigung*—[76]

INGE. I was asking, if you catch Paul you won't slay him, will you?

HESS. Frau Zauritz, my mind really hurts hearing that question. I have a boy too. A wife.

STRUBBEL. You're writing a letter to your wife?

HESS (*embarrassed*). Yes.

STRUBBEL. How is she?

HESS. She's fallen really alone. The boy's gone off to the army, really alone. Here, look at this photo—(*shows everyone*) lives in Rostock. Look, strolling on the seaside—really alone—

STRUBBEL. Alone? Then who took the picture?

(*Startled, Hess looks at the picture, then laughs once with a worried face.*)

HESS. That's right?

---

76 'I beg to be excused.'

(*At Justice Voss' entrance, everyone stands.*)

VOSS. Sit. I've called you to a specially important session. Helga!

(*Helga enters.*)

A report has to be written.

(*Helga sits.*)

The Huettig case is about to take an unexpected turn. It's better to hear about it in this secret session, before the public law court. Herr Landt, there's a reporter named Otto Birkholz in your newspaper.

LANDT. Yes, Herr General.

VOSS. In a lengthy petition he has let me know some startling facts about the Huettig case. After reading that petition I have no doubts that he ought to be called as a witness.

LANDT (*alarmed*). Herr General, think over whether you ought to or not.

VOSS (*forcefully*). Herr Landt, do you think yourself equal to a Justice? I have no doubts that Herr Birkholz's testimony is necessary. Helga, call him.[77]

(*Otto enters, some papers in his hand.*)

Your name? Profession?

OTTO. Otto Birkholz, reporter for the *Freie Zeitung* paper.

VOSS. Did you write me a petition about the Huettig case?

OTTO. Yes.

VOSS. Your petition has been accepted. Speak whatever you have to say. You can also question whoever you wish. Captain Hess, you can interrogate the witness.

---

77 In the video, Helga exits and reenters, preceding Otto.

OTTO. Honourable Justice, what I'm about to do here was not my work. I had received instructions to write about this case from our paper's perspective. Our honourable editor, especially, is an exceptional devotee of truth. He has a watch. That watch is his prize for fearless truthfulness. He showed me that watch and said—

VOSS. There's no need for irrelevance.

OTTO. This is the relevance. My sudden advent as witness is due to this relevance. He said, 'Speak the truth, not for fear of anyone, for the interests of the paper's ideals.' That became my ruin. From the goadings of truthfulness I suddenly saw some discrepancies in Mrs Zauritz's deposition. Mrs Zauritz, you told me, the killers screamed at the time of knifing, 'Long live the Communist Party!' My question: Would they entangle themselves in this manner in a case of killing? They'd smash their own jar?

HESS. Communists behave like that.

OTTO. The second question, Mrs Zauritz: What did the driver say on getting into the car?

INGE. *Wo muss ich einbiegen, Kamerad?* Which way will I turn at the corner, comrade?

OTTO. What did you determine from this?

INGE. I understood they were Communists, otherwise why would they call each other *kamerad*?

OTTO. But do you know that Communists no longer call each other *kamerad*? (*Commotion*) I mixed with them and with my own ears heard them say *genosse*. I've brought more news; they dropped the word *kamerad* from their dictionary ten years ago.

HESS. Do you want to say that Mrs Zauritz spoke a lie?

OTTO. No, she's saying the truth. And if she says the truth, it's proven that the people in the car weren't Communists, but people from some other circle. Then Doctor Strubbel, when you saw the tall person striking Herr Zauritz with knife blows, what did Zauritz say?

STRUBBEL. I've said all that in court.

VOSS. Say it again.

STRUBBEL. '*Warum schlachten Sie mich.*'[78] Why do you slay me?

OTTO. Yet Frau Zauritz told me, Richard Huettig was an object of dear affection for the dead Zauritz.

INGE. Yes, I did.

HESS. What's proved by that? An object of affection can't stab?

OTTO. He can, but will anyone call an object of affection so formally? Frau Zauritz, did your husband call Huettig *du* or *Sie*?[79]

INGE. They're my boy's friends—he called him *du*.

OTTO. But the knife-wounded Zauritz said to the tall person: '*Warum schlachten* Sie *mich?*'

STRUBBEL. That's what I heard, but I'm not in any political dispute.

OTTO. No, no, you're a venerable individual, you're speaking the truth. But if you spoke the truth, then it's proved that the tall person wasn't Huettig, it was someone else, someone Zauritz wasn't acquainted with. Then—the police had presented a leaflet. Captain Hess, you have a copy of it.

HESS. Certainly. Here you are.

OTTO. Where did you find the leaflet?

HESS. The Communist Party office. There are witnesses.

---

78 In the video, Strubbel raises his hand and shouts loudly, dramatically, exactly like he did in Scene Four.

79 Dutt adds another line here using the Bengali equivalents, for Bengali has the same distinction between the pronouns *tumi* (informal) and *āpni* (formal).

OTTO. Read the last bit.

HESS. 'The Red Guards of the labourers' army are ready. Ernst Telman, General Secretary, Communist Party of Germany.'

OTTO. This is a genuine Communist leaflet?

HESS. Seems so to me.

OTTO. Captain Hess, don't the Communists know their Secretary's name?

HESS. Meaning?

OTTO. Ernst Telman was appointed to the party's chairmanship one year ago.[80] Their present secretary's name is Martin Scher. This is somewhat inconvenient for outsiders to know, because the party leaders have gone into hiding and the reshuffling of posts was done secretly. But it's not believable that Communists themselves won't know who's their General Secretary, so it seems to me that this leaflet's forged and those who have done this crude forgery are raw forgers, they don't keep well up on the news. This was my submission, Herr Richter.

(Commotion; everyone talks together.)

VOSS. *Hören Sie.*[81] Stop the commotion.

HESS. How did you know about the Communist Party's internal matters? Do you have a secret membership?

OTTO. No. I know all this after mixing with them for the past ten days.

HESS. Is it doing good to mix with them in these circumstances?

VOSS *(bellows)*. Captain Hess! Are you threatening the witness in front of me?

---

80 In fact, Thälmann had become chairman in 1925. In 1932, he was the Communist candidate for the presidency.

81 'Listen.'

•

HESS. I beg forgiveness. But will the witness say why blood was found on Huettig's knife and coat?

VOSS. Irrelevant. My impression is that's another case. The police have not proved whose blood it is. Is there any path except acquitting Huettig in this case as not guilty?

(*Lippert enters.*)

LIPPERT. *Entschuldigen Sie bitte.* (*Gives a paper to Hess.*)[82]

VOSS. Come this side. (*Explains to Lippert the new circumstances of the case.*)

INGE. Otto, come this side. You know, you've dispelled my nightmare?

OTTO. Nightmare?

INGE. Yes. That my boy could kill my husband—you've suddenly freed me from this curse. I thank you. I'm grateful to you on Paul's behalf too. Oof, how foolish of me. I was blind.

LANDT. Your job's gone. If you enter our office again, I'll bash you up.

STRUBBEL. You've thrown me in acute danger. If the Nazis now say Huettig got acquitted for me?

(*Helga brings large bottles of beer and sets them down.*)[83]

STRUBBEL. Listen, do you have acetylsalicylic acid?

HELGA. What's that?

LANDT. Aspirin, aspirin.

STRUBBEL. Yes, aspirin. Never remember it.

HELGA. You never remember aspirin, but remember that huge word?

---

82 The Complete Plays omits Lippert's line and the stage direction. I have reinstated them from the first edition (also confirmed by the video).

83 In the video, Helga does not perform this stage direction, no doubt in deference to Voss' presence.

STRUBBEL. I'm a doctor.

(*Seeing the seated Otto writing something, Landt bursts out.*)

LANDT. What are you writing so furiously? Now what destruction are you doing me?

OTTO. No, no, I'm writing a report of what just happened. It'll come out in tomorrow's paper.

LANDT. *Nein! Niemals.*[84] All that won't be printed. Your job's already gone. Why are you sweating your head about what will or won't come out in my paper?

OTTO. No way my job can go. If I lose my job, I'll tangle you in this up to your neck. I'll say you told me to turn the case around by searching out facts. In the interests of truth, your written directive is with me.

LANDT. Are you threatening me?

OTTO. Certainly. You created all this by showing me that watch.

LANDT. Come this side. (*Taking him aside*) You can't understand my . . . my problem. I've fallen into a botheration.

OTTO. What botheration?

LANDT.[85] Listen, at the time of the past World War, I'd committed an indiscretion. Tempted by money, I'd supplied some classified facts to the American government.

OTTO. So you did it for money? You did well.

LANDT. Ah, why don't you listen. All those documents are now in the Nazis' hands. They . . . they are threatening me—if my paper doesn't come down to Nazi electoral publicity fully,

---

84 'No! Never.' In the video, Landt first nods to Otto in assent and then does a double-take before he says this.

85 The Complete Plays names Inge as the speaker. Obviously these lines belong to Landt, following the first edition.

then . . . then they'll publish all those facts and . . . arrest me on grounds of, what's it called, sedition.

OTTO. That's what I said. Why has the *Freie Zeitung*, impartial worshipper of truth, suddenly descended to such a part as royal page? Of course, my wife did say—

LANDT.[86] For the past one month I haven't slept one full night. What should I do?

INGE (*coming forward*). What can you do? With headlines as big as those which said the Communists were killers, say that the Communists are blameless. Nobody will mind at all. Everyone's accustomed to seeing your somersaults.

LANDT. No, Frau Zauritz, you don't know all, so—

(*Voss and Lippert end their discussion—*)

LIPPERT. Captain Hess, after this the police will withdraw the case of course?

HESS. Of course.

VOSS. Then tomorrow morning I'll acquit Huettig as not guilty. Present Huettig at ten in the morning.

HESS. That won't be possible anymore, Herr General. The Central[87] Feldpolizei has taken Huettig away as prisoner under the Security Act[88]. He's now in the Central Ploetzensee Prison. We have no hand in it anymore.

---

86 In the video, Landt begins with 'Keep your wife out of this.'

87 Actually Geheime: Secret, not Central, military police. This is anachronistic because the Geheime Feldpolizei had been disbanded after World War I; Hitler reinstated it, but not so soon after coming to power.

88 The Reichstag Fire Decree for Protection, the first of Hitler's repressive measures, became law only on 28 February 1933, followed immediately by widespread arrests of Communists. See the beginning of Scene Eight. Clearly Dutt composed this sentence about the police and the Act to create greater dramatic impact.

(*Quivering in tremendous anger, Voss comes forward.*)

INGE (*shouting*). Huettig's blameless. I, Zauritz's wife, say Richard Huettig's blameless. By what right will you keep him captive?

VOSS. Herr Lippert, do you know anything about this shameless interference in the rights of the Justice Department?

LIPPERT. Yes, Herr General, this has happened by Prime Minister Hitler's instructions.

VOSS. You take captive a sub-judice prisoner from in front of the Justice?

LIPPERT. Huettig's a dangerous person, Herr General.

VOSS. Huettig's not dangerous, his appearance in the court is dangerous, Justice Voss is dangerous, the court itself is dangerous, the only fear is your forgery will be caught. It will be caught, Herr Lippert. You still don't know Justice Voss. You won't be able to cover up this case by spiriting Huettig away.

LIPPERT. Herr Richter, don't put any blame on me. I had tried— had tried—(*quivering violently*) I'm unwell—

VOSS. You are a forger. Captain Hess is a liar. This whole case was set up as an electoral move. The impression is also dawning on me that Zauritz was killed by either plainclothes police or your Nazi goons' group. A Justice ought not to make all these political comments. I never have, but now that I understand you people don't honour the purity of law, you want to throttle justice, I am compelled to open my mouth. If you appear at the court, you'll hear what I say.

EIGHT

In the distance, Hitler's image becomes visible again[89]. He is speechifying in front of a row of mikes.

HITLER. You've seen with your own eyes, we make no lapses in trying to keep the coming elections unobstructed and free. But the Communist Party won't let that happen. Last night[90] someone or some people set fire to the Berlin Reichstag. One individual was arrested red-handed at the scene. His name is van der Lubbe.[91] A Dutch Communist Party member's card was in his pocket. The Communist Party wants to put German democracy in the grave by setting fire to the legislative assembly building. As Chancellor I am compelled to accept some unavoidable measures: (1) the Communist Party is declared verboten; (2) a directive is issued to arrest members of that party on sight and if necessary to shoot them to death on sight. (3) From today all forms of trade-union activities are verboten. (4) From today all forms of farmers' associations are verboten. (5) From today all forms of political, economic agitations by government employees and students are verboten. The 5 March elections will be held, the Communists don't have the ability to foil them, but, apart from[92]

---

89 As the video confirms, through a scrim in the middle of the huge newspaper backdrop as in Scene Five.

90 27 February 1933. Hitler appears not to have made such a speech the following day, though he got President Hindenburg to sign the Reichstag Fire Decree. The measures unfolded gradually over the next few weeks.

91 Marinus van der Lubbe, guillotined in prison in 1934. Recent historians implicate the Nazis in conspiring to burn down the Reichstag and blaming it on the Communists.

92 The Complete Plays deletes 'apart from' by mistake, suggesting that all rights are suspended.

electoral rights, all other citizens' rights are temporarily suspended on account of the emergency situation. Inhabitants of Germany. Vote for the Nazi Party on 5 March. Establish socialism in Germany.

(A couple of disconcerting scenes of Stormtrooper expeditions through Berlin thoroughfares manifest themselves in front of us. We see them come rushing with swastika-emblazoned flags in hand, bellowing, throwing bricks targeted at a window, pulling Rudolf out and giving him tremendous beatings.[93] *While imploring, Rudolf falls flat on his face; beatings continue relentlessly. Then they hold his legs and drag his body away. On the backdrop, flames of fire. From the wings, the noise of shooting, shouting, Nazi slogans and sirens.)*

* * *

(In Justice Voss' private chamber, Inge and Otto sitting as before. And Landt pacing excitedly. Outside, repeatedly, the noises of shouting and shooting.)

LANDT. You call this elections? You call this democracy? It's a farce! There's a farce on outside. Standing before the barrel of a gun, the populace will give independent views, will they!

INGE. Why get so excited, Herr Landt? Sit down!

---

93 They do not drag Rudolf out in the video: Rudolf appears at the barricade later. Instead, they place a placard saying 'Jew' round the neck of a man and shoot him. Actor Samir Majumdar confirms that this episode existed in the original production, and that the Jew was the Professor mentioned in the Dramatis Personae, who does not have any other appearance in the play. Then the Stormtroopers drag Paul in and beat him. Finally, Communist workers led by a woman unfolding the Red flag take weapons out and prepare to fight.

LANDT. Frau Zauritz, I've stayed in the Charlottenburg area now for 32 years. I've voted in each election. I couldn't today.

INGE. Why?

LANDT. A group of goons stood with guns in hand. They said, your vote's been cast, go away. I'm powerless to exercise my sacred voting rights.

(*Inge and Otto laugh.*)

INGE. But you too are at the root of losing sacred voting rights in this manner.

LANDT. Meaning?

INGE. You raised such an uproar—saying finish off the Communists, that the Nazis . . . came out on the roads with guns.

LANDT. But I'd have voted for the Nazis. They didn't understand.

INGE (*laughing*). Then why scream any more? Your vote's fallen into their box, after all. See how convenient. You don't have to make an effort to go out in this March wind—you sit at home, and on that side the vote falls.

LANDT. But my sacred right (*the words get lost in the noise of machineguns*) What's this, who's firing machineguns?

INGE. Police.

LANDT. Why are they in this?

INGE. Don't you know they're surrounding localities, to slay? The police come and surround, the Nazis enter afterwards and search for Communists. Sitting at my window I see them standing boys in a row and shooting them. At some time afterwards they raise their pistols and say: Close your windows. Then I close them.

OTTO. Yesterday they surrounded the Moabit locality, slew one and a half thousand people. There were girls, children, the old among them.

LANDT. They're Communists, so they'll be slain.

INGE. Communists? All trade unions are verboten, farmers' associations, students' agitations are verboten, those are still the slogans. Even if we chop off this person's head he'll go to market to buy a new hat.[94] He doesn't even understand what he's losing.

LANDT. Justice Voss still hasn't come. I have lots of work. (*Looks at his watch*)

OTTO. That watch doesn't suit your hand anymore. Sell it off.

(*Strubbel enters at tremendous speed, clothes torn, hair dishevelled. Blood streaming from forehead. Behind him, Bauer, Mueller and Kurt.*)

KURT. Halt! *Warum laufen Sie so?* Why're you running like this? Extremely suspicious.

BAUER. *Bitte folgen Sie uns zur Wache.*[95] You have to go to the police station.

INGE. Listen, we know him, he's a famous doctor—

KURT. You stay away. Why did you come running? Why's there blood on your forehead? Where are you coming from?

STRUBBEL. I'm coming from in front of Humboldt University!

MUELLER. Why did you run?

STRUBBEL. They were hitting me.

MUELLER. Who?

STRUBBEL. You people.

KURT. Us?

---

94 She directs this line at Landt, who reacts instinctively by feeling the top of his head.

95 'Please follow us to the police station.'

STRUBBEL. I mean everyone in that uniform looks the same. Your colleagues. The Stormtroopers.

KURT. Why did they come to hit you? What had you done?

STRUBBEL. I'd gone for their own good. Herr Landt, bring out your notebook, write it down, it'll make good headlines. Book-burning festival under Goebbels' supervision in front of Humboldt University![96] A new event in free, civilized Germany.

LANDT. Book-burning festival?

STRUBBEL. Yes, Marx and Engels were being burnt to ashes anyway, in the end when I saw the fates of Thomas Mann[97], Erich Maria Remarque and Heinrich Heine set on fire too, I said just once in a faint voice: It doesn't look good to leave out Goethe and Schiller[98], then those cultured Germans began to assault me. And I fled.

KURT. What's your name, your profession?

INGE. He's injured, have you absolutely abandoned kindness and compassion? Let him sit.

KURT (forcefully). Don't poke your nose into this. Name?

STRUBBEL. Hermann Strubbel, I'm a doctor.

KURT. Let's see your pass.

(Strubbel keeps groping inside his pockets, then takes a book out, gives it to Kurt and gropes his pockets once more.)

What's this?

---

96 The infamous incident led by Joseph Goebbels, Nazi Minister of Propaganda, occurred later, on 10 May 1933.

97 In fact, Goebbels named Heinrich Mann, Thomas's brother and anti-fascist author.

98 Strubbel says 'Shakespeare' instead of 'Schiller' in the video, no doubt for the instant recognition of spectators.

STRUBBEL. The Bible. While I search for the pass, you can glance through that, it's a good book. (*Searches again*) Of course, it's written by Jews but ought it to be burnt? Here's the pass.

KURT (*holding his collar*).[99] *Morgen werden Sie einen grossen Muskelkater haben.*[100] Come, I see you still haven't been educated.

MUELLER. Kurt? That won't be needed. He's a famous doctor.

KURT. I can't tolerate famous doctors and physicians. Writers, doctors, lawyers—all parasites. They have to be pulled up by the roots one by one. Stand them at road corners and whip them.

MUELLER (*forcefully*). All those are hoodlums' words. Release him.

(*Kurt thinks of something; then takes Bauer out with him. Mueller seats Strubbel; Inge comes forward intending to nurse him.*)

INGE (*to Mueller*). Why have you joined their group? You won't be able to keep in step with them. In the end you'll die too.

MUELLER. I entered due to my stomach. I have no job, so I entered. And I detest Communists, so I entered!

OTTO. What harm have Communists done to you?

MUELLER. It's they who demolished everything. Enraged labourers to close down factories—

OTTO. And the factory owners are blameless?

MUELLER. All that I don't know. Pushed by the Communists' stoppages, all factories are closing down. So we're unemployed.

INGE. Is there any workman on earth who goes on stoppage unless compelled? You were a labourer. Tell me, does anyone play with his own livelihood?

---

99 Instead, in the video he throws the Bible on the floor.
100 'Tomorrow morning you'll have a major muscle ache.'

MUELLER (*suddenly*). I don't know all that. The Communists are agents of the Soviet Union. They have to be slain, period.

INGE. If you can slay them, you'll get a reward too.

MUELLER. What?

INGE. The owners give baksheesh. That's your politics. The politics of cash. I've killed four boys, master, therefore at twenty marks per head my dues are eighty marks.

OTTO. And otherwise collecting donations by threatening people of the neighbourhood, then drinking and gambling. You're the warriors of German independence against the Soviet Union? Makes me laugh.

MUELLER (*shouting*). You know what the pains of unemployment are? Have you ever seen your brothers and sisters panting from hunger? Swine, son of a rich man! I wish I could—punch you and pulp your face—

(*Lippert and Hess enter. Mueller goes out quickly.*[101])

LIPPERT. Forgive us, we got delayed. The toil on the occasion of elections—

INGE. What more toil, Herr Lippert, in these elections you don't have any rivals.

LIPPERT. Truly, Frau Zauritz, a really sorrowful incident occurred. Why did they suddenly go and set fire to the legislative assembly?

INGE. Since the Zauritz murder backfired.

LIPPERT. What are you saying?

INGE. I'm saying, the Zauritz murder couldn't be placed on the Communists' shoulders. So, in order to help you, they put party cards in their pockets and went to set fire to the legislative assembly. If this too doesn't work, they'll wrap red ensigns

---

101 And Strubbel hides behind Landt in the video.

round their bodies and try to kill Hitler. I see the Communists are prepared to lay down their lives in order to help you.

LIPPERT (*laughing*). I acknowledge there's appropriate cause for your irony. (*Seeing Strubbel*) What's happened to him?

STRUBBEL. No, no, nothing's happened. I've rubbed red paint on my forehead in play. Further, you'll be delighted to hear, I didn't even go to vote. As it is I heard that 2,000 more votes than the total number of votes at our booth had been cast in the morning. I didn't go to create any further hindrance among all these invisible, disembodied extra voters. Let me stay a little unpublicized.

LIPPERT (*seeing Landt*). Herr Landt, you're here? You haven't gone to office.

LANDT (*with a wide smile*). No, Herr Lippert, I've come here at Justice Voss' directive. He said he'll give that statement—

LIPPERT. But you ought to have gone to office—especially when your paper's in such a crisis.

LANDT (*sore-throated in alarm*). What crisis?

HESS. What's that! Haven't you heard? Under special powers the government today has made the publication of eleven newspapers verboten. Among them is the *Freie Zeitung*.

(*From Landt's voice a grief-stricken shout issues forth. Inge, Strubbel and Otto laugh out.*)

LANDT. *Freie Zeitung*! Why *Freie Zeitung*, is my paper a Communist Party paper?

HESS. No, why that?

LANDT. Then?

LIPPERT. Herr Landt, when a race stands as one behind a leader, naturally it talks to one tune. It doesn't allow any scope then for tunelessness.

LANDT. But I'm in that tune, I'm not tuneless. I've been regularly printing your words in bold black letters. I haven't released one paper recently without committing the Communist Party's funeral. I've continuously printed Hitler's pictures. Whatever you've told me on the telephone I've printed on the front page verbatim, saying: Despatched by our own correspondent. My paper's virtually become the Nazi Party's mouthpiece.

LIPPERT. That's not enough. We can't leave any opportunity for singing contrarily in future. When the country has awoken, when in the not-so-distant future Germany's victorious pennant will have to fly on foreign battlefields, when Moscow will have to be ground under German boots, everything in the country will be regulated by the finger-pointing of one leader. We can't keep all those 'fearless' periodicals impartial to groups and views.

LANDT. Those are words for words' sake. I print them since I have to. Sir, couldn't you consider it a little?

LIPPERT. Consideration's not in my hands, it's in the Fuehrer's.

INGE. The elections still aren't over. Already this? What'll happen afterwards?

(*Landt has sat down with hand on his head. Suddenly he says—*)

LANDT. Once I called Stalin a son of a bitch on the front page, upon your orders.

LIPPERT (*in a momentarily harsh tone*). Herr Landt. If you repeatedly mention my orders, my telephone and so on, we too will publish your actual nature to the public eye.

LANDT (*shudders but cannot stop*). And once I wrote, Communists enjoy each other's wives—that too on your—(*Landt covers his own mouth and stops.*)

LIPPERT. Now let's come to work matters. In a special instruction the government says Huettig's case has to continue, whatever the result may be. Captain Hess, the police won't be allowed to withdraw the case. The Nazi Party won't condone your closing the case and escaping as soon as you're inconvenienced.

HESS. Fine, the case will continue.

LIPPERT. The government has issued another instruction notifying Georg Teichert as Justice for this case.

INGE. What's that? Without Justice Voss this case can't continue.

STRUBBEL. The government doesn't have the right to remove Voss.

LIPPERT. Why should the government remove Voss? Haven't you heard?

HESS. Justice Voss has been heinously killed today at dawn? (*Everyone shudders.*) There's enough cause to suspect that the Communists, perturbed by the possible result of the case, murdered him. The police are investigating.

(*Silence for a while.*)

INGE. Where, how was he killed?

HESS. Every day at dawn he went for a stroll by the side of Mueggelsee lake. Today some people shot and murdered him there.

INGE. And didn't those people scream 'Long live the Communist Party'?

(*Silence. Then—*)

HESS. No, Frau Zauritz. However, there are eyewitnesses. They have identified two renowned Communists.

LIPPERT. Therefore the case will continue under Justice Teichert's jurisdiction.

INGE. Doesn't Albert Voss have a wife?

HESS. Voss was a widower. His wife died five years ago.

INGE. She was saved.

LIPPERT. According to law, the case will begin again from the start. We have a question about this for Herr Otto Birkholz. Does he want to be a witness for this case? We're getting ready a list of witnesses. We'll keep your name, right?

(*Otto can't even understand fully where there's a veiled threat.*)

OTTO. Yes, it seems to me, my testimony's very urgent.

LIPPERT. Captain Hess, write down his name. Address?

(*Gradually, Otto starts sweating.*)

OTTO. What about my address? If you send it to the address of the *Freie Zeitung* paper—no, that's not there either.

LIPPERT. Address, Herr Birkholz?

(*Otto does not answer.*)

HESS. In your deposition you repeatedly spoke of mixing with the Communists. Will you receive letters sent to the Charlotten-burg Communist Party office address?

LIPPERT. It's not there either? That office was set ablaze today. Herr Birkholz, address?

OTTO. I've thought it over, I won't be a witness in this case. I mean—I've got lots of work—won't have time.

LIPPERT. Captain Hess, strike out his name. He can't be present because he's busy with various work. Doctor Strubbel?

STRUBBEL. No, no, I have a terrible workload. I have to see patients. Besides, I have to read books. I mean those books that aren't being burnt, what else? Good books. Such as Hitler's autobiography.

LIPPERT (*laughing*). If all of you behave like this, then how will the case continue? You're an eyewitness. You'll have to give testimony?

STRUBBEL. Of course, of course I'll have to give testimony. Even amid hundreds of other work, that's a duty, the national duty. Address, 115 Wallstrasse.

HESS. Shall we file your earlier deposition this time too?

STRUBBEL. Herr Lippert, what do you say?

LIPPERT. What will I say? You understand your deposition. Do you have anything new to say?

STRUBBEL. No, no, are you mad? That deposition stays.

LIPPERT. Frau Zauritz, you're an eyewitness too. You'll give testimony, certainly?

INGE. Certainly.

HESS. We know your address. We'll file the earlier deposition, right?

INGE. No. This time the deposition's completely different. I'll file it later.

(*Silence*)

LIPPERT. What new facts do you know that you'll change the deposition?

INGE. You have no right at all to ask this question.

LIPPERT. Forgive me for the unrightful practice.

HESS. You'll identify Huettig in court this time too?

INGE. No.

OTTO. Frau Zauritz, think a little over what you're doing.

HESS. You won't identify him?

INGE. How will I? I've got to know all. There's no point glaring at me with bloodshot eyes, Captain Hess. I'm too dangerous a witness, I know too much. But do one thing. Perhaps I don't go at dawn for a stroll by the lakeside, but I stay completely alone at home—there won't be any lack of opportunity.

STRUBBEL (*in undertones*). Frau Zauritz! What are you doing!

INGE. A little courage, Dr Strubbel, a little courage is needed. Straighten the spine a little and speak eyeball to eyeball. A little courage is a spark, you know? It can light a fire.

LIPPERT. Frau Zauritz, we won't interfere in your independent views at court—[102]

INGE. No, before that. You'll kill—I mean the Communists will suddenly come, kill me and go.

LIPPERT. Nobody will lay a hand on you—and, I'm unwell—you see this leg trembling constantly, I can't stop it. It doesn't obey discipline any more. My limbs (*screaming*) are rebels, hands and legs are rebelling—no one will tell you anything, but— Bauer! Bring him in.

(*Kurt, Mueller and Bauer drag in the bloody, almost unconscious Paul. Everyone stands up and gathers. On Inge's stone-like face, only the eyes stay wide open in disbelief.*)

HESS. Paul Schall was caught last night. At the time of arrest he fired. Therefore, according to the Fuehrer's directive, he could be shot to death in retaliatory fire.

LIPPERT. Frau . . . Frau . . . Zauritz, this violent creature killed your husband . . . therefore you're certainly . . . very . . . very pleased to see this scene.

HESS (*to Paul*). Where's Franz Zander? Where's Bruno?

PAUL. I don't know.

LIPPERT. Actually—oof, this time the whole body's trembling— actually he knows all—

(*Kurt and Bauer hit Paul with steel whips.*)

---

102 This line and Inge's response (both restored from the first edition) are inexplicably missing in the Complete Plays.

PAUL. Don't know—don't know—don't know.

INGE (*the intense pain in the eyes doesn't match at all with the calm tone*). You're all deranged. You're the end of civilization. You're crucifying Jesus again.

LIPPERT. Ca-Ca-Captain Hess, take him outside, and according to the Fuehrer's directive No. 2—shoot him—him to death. We'll never be able to do that much in front of the mother.

(*Taking out his pistol, Hess leaves; Kurt and Bauer pull Paul out.*)

INGE. Herr Lippert, don't slay my boy.

LIPPERT. He-he-he killed your husband—

INGE. Herr Lippert, don't slay Paul. Whatever you tell me to say in court, I'll say it, don't slay Paul.

LIPPERT. *Wunderbar!*[103] Mueller, tell Captain Hess that Paul Schall must not be slain.

(*Mueller runs as if his life depends on it—but even before he departs, the noise of bullets outside. Mueller goes out. Quivering, Lippert goes to the door—turns and says—*)

You left it too late. (*A heartrending shout comes out from Inge's voice.*) *Moerder! Assassine!*[104] Sons of killer police! They're rebelling, they don't hear my words. . . . My whole form's trembling, see, I haven't any hand in it.

(*Exit.*)

INGE. Josef. You ought not to return home so late at night. You won't be able to bear such hard labour, besides the times aren't good—

---

103 'Wonderful!'
104 'Murderer! Assassin!'

(*With anxious faces, Strubbel and Otto come forward towards Inge. But avoiding their hands, Inge comes forward. As she speaks, everyone else disappears from view.*)

Then discipline Paul; tell me, why has talk between you stopped? . . . Shouldn't I see it? You enter the room he goes out, as soon as he enters you leave in anger . . . What's this, why are your shoes in this condition? No, no, I'm wiping them. What will people say if you go outside in this condition? They'll say the old woman doesn't look after the old man any more—

(*Sitting in front of an armchair, she starts cleaning shoes; as soon as she raises her face she sees Paul standing like Jesus in a white robe and with a crown of thorns on his head.*)

Paul, when did you come?

PAUL. Just now.

INGE. How many days haven't you eaten, tell me.

PAUL. I get to eat, there's no lack of food. Sleep's what I don't have. When will I sleep, tell me? I don't lie down for two nights running in the same house.

INGE. Sleepless Jesus doesn't have a place to rest his head. Birds in the sky have nests, jackals have holes, but the Son of Man doesn't have place to rest his head. Paul, how many days will you continue in this manner? Won't your health break down?

PAUL (*with a smile-filled face, in a calm tone*). I haven't come to distribute peace. I've come to create rifts between father and son, brother and brother. I've come to give the sword.[105]

---

105 I have rendered the Bengali into English, but the lines echo the Bible, Matthew 10:34–35, where Jesus speaks of a social schism that cleaves even family bonds.

INGE. Ah, that's good, you've still got the Bible memorized.

PAUL. You hit me so at the time of learning it, do I have any way of forgetting it? Mother, where's that pistol of Father's?

INGE. It's there. In the big chest in the attic.

PAUL. Bring it down! What are you doing? Bring it, clean it, load bullets into it.

INGE. That . . . that's a weapon, what will I do with it?

PAUL. Shoot. What else will you do?

INGE. Will I be able to shoot someone with a cool head?

(*We can see, standing at a barricade on Wallstrasse, with bloody bodies, torn clothes, Zander, Bruno, Heinz Preuss and Willi—guns in hand. Inge stands in front of them with her husband's pistol. Otto too stands on one side.*)

ZANDER. Then why did you come, Frau Zauritz? Why did you come here if you can't shoot with a cool head?

INGE. I'll have to try. (*Bruno laughs out.*) No, no, why do you laugh? I'll have to try. They're dragging out boys and girls from their homes onto the roads and slaying them, I'll have to fire a pistol. Even if I can't fire it, I can load bullets into your guns. I mean I can do that work if someone just shows me.

BRUNO. Okay. Bruno will teach you. (*To Otto*) Well, why are you here? To take an interview or what? Then write—the stratagem of indiscriminate murder after surrounding a neighbourhood has failed in Wallstrasse. Till today twenty-one—meaning a score and one attacks have been pulverized at the Wallstrasse barricade. This time tanks will probably arrive.

OTTO. No, I've brought her—and despite my wife forbidding me, I've resolved to fight.

ZANDER. Why?

OTTO. They'll slay me, of course. Like an ignorant, I've poked my nose too much into the Huettig case. So where else do I hide?

ZANDER. You know anything about fighting?

OTTO (*standing at attention*). In the last war I was a soldier, Brandenburg Brigade, soldier number 638712, Herr Lieutenant.

ZANDER (*laughing*). Over there's your position.

INGE (*pulling a large bag*). I've brought food for you all. I mean, what little there was at home.

HEINZ. You've saved us. We've had no food for two days.

BRUNO.[106] You came with such a big package on your shoulders? Couldn't they see you? If they had, they'd have shot you, do you know?

ZANDER. Frau Zauritz, do you know that two or four barricades like this have no point, our deaths are inevitable?

INGE. Yes.

BRUNO.[107] Then why did you come here to die?

INGE. I understood after seeing a lot—a lot of things, that to die standing up is better than to survive kneeling down. (*While eating, the Communists look up amazed*) I'm not a Communist, I don't know anything except Jesus. So I used to say at the beginning—they're slaying a few Communists, what's it to us? Now I understand, the Communists die first, then the others' turns come one by one, then—then one day I see the entire country's a jailhouse.

---

106 These lines are spoken by the woman Communist in the video (performed as a double role by the same actress who played Helga in the Dramatis Personae, which mistakenly identifies Helga as 'Communist worker'). In the first edition, the speech heading here is inadvertently 'Madhu', a Bengali name.

107 In the video and the first edition, spoken by the woman/Madhu.

WILLI. *Halt.* Come with hands over your head!

(*Dr Strubbel enters in front of everyone's raised rifles and crosses the barricade.*)

INGE. Dr Strubbel, with what on your mind have you come here?

STRUBBEL. And with what on your mind have you come here?

ZANDER. Doctor, have you come to fight a war or what?

STRUBBEL. War! Will I be able to fight a war? War doesn't come to me easily.

BRUNO. Then what do you want here?

STRUBBEL. Where else will I go? I didn't—what do they say—get along well with the Nazis.

INGE. It would have been fine if you'd given testimony in the Huettig case like a bright child.

STRUBBEL. I couldn't do that. Suddenly I felt quite ashamed.

INGE. Ashamed of what?

STRUBBEL. An educated man's self-reproach, what else. (*He paces*) If I have to survive by carrying out their commands, where's my respect for reading Schopenhauer and Karl Marx? They're burning books, understand?

OTTO. I'd told you earlier, an educated man ought to have views.

STRUBBEL. Yes. But when you told me, did I know that views themselves would become illegal? Yesterday they attacked a theatre in Schiffbauerdamm. (*Pacing*) If we have to save education and inspiration, wisdom and intelligence, knowledge and science—then—what do I say?

INGE. Then you'll have to come to the barricade and stand behind these Brunos, is that it?

STRUBBEL. Yes.

BRUNO. But you say war doesn't come to you, what will you do here?

STRUBBEL. Some other work. (*Sits, immediately rises*) Oof, what dust.[108] Suppose, during the lulls in the war I can recite Goethe's poems to you. That will increase your morale.

INGE. And during the lulls in reciting poetry you can learn to fire a rifle, Doctor, otherwise how will your morale increase?

BRUNO. Hey you, haven't you brought a camera?

OTTO. No.

BRUNO. Then I'd have asked you to take a picture of this lady.[109]

HEINZ. You believe in Jesus, then why get tangled in killing?

INGE (*in a proud voice*). I haven't come to distribute peace, I've come to give the sword. (*Embarrassed laugh*) Why don't you read the Bible, son? I also believe this now—the last judgment comes through bullets from a gun. You'll have to say all there is to say by flashing fire from the barrel of a gun. They won't understand any other language.

BRUNO (*booming laugh*). *Genossin* Zauritz—notice we don't say *Kamerad*—*Genossin*, you know more than this Franz ape. (*About to laugh again but starts gasping*)

INGE. What happened?

BRUNO. A bullet struck my chest day before—

(*Inge busy nursing*)

ZANDER. Don't laugh any more, by Mary, you'll die.

INGE. Oh, what a condition your chest's in. (*Silence, Inge is cleansing the wound, suddenly—*) All right, do any of you keep contact with Clara? Clara Grunberg.

---

108 Everyone laughs in the video.

109 In the video, Bruno says instead, 'Then I'd have asked you to take a photograph of this grand barricade as a witness to history.'

HEINZ. You mean Paul's um—dame?

ZANDER. He's done it.[110]

BRUNO. Our trade's with all these base people! Hey lamey, get up.[111] You're asking after Paul's betrothed or beloved or— um—that girlie, right?

ZANDER. What polite language.[112]

INGE. Yes.

BRUNO. No contact at all. Now let me go, I have to get up.

INGE. Lie down quietly.

BRUNO. Eh, no, no, they won't be able to fight without me. If I'm not there that Franz bastard will forget the fight and make love with this dame perhaps—

ZANDER. You're mocking me?[113] (*Laughing*) You're illegitimate. (*Immediately, seeing the lady present, covers his mouth*)

---

110 Replaced in the video with: 'Say "lady".'

111 In the video, Bruno's speech after this goes: 'You don't know the language in which you ought to talk to a lady. Let me speak. Frau Zauritz, you . . . you're asking after Paul's beloved . . . no, not beloved, their relationship was closer—because their marriage had been fixed . . . you're asking after Paul's betrothed . . . no, not betrothed, their relationship was closer—because their union had been consummated in bed. So, Frau Zauritz, you're asking after Paul's whore?' Dutt used to enact Bruno himself and could carry off these lines with his customary aplomb.

112 Spoken by the Communist woman in the video (Madhu in the first edition).

113 In the video, the woman (Madhu in the first edition) asks 'You're mocking me?' and Bruno continues, 'And if I'm not there that Rudolf you see there will guzzle and empty all the liquor in his own shop.' Then Rudolf retorts by uttering Zander's next imprecation.

BRUNO. This is their education and inspiration. They're foul-mouthed in front of you. And this lamey—if I'm not at his side he can't shoot bullets.

HEINZ. Go on, don't keep jabbering—

BRUNO. Without me they're orphaned. (*To Otto*) I mean underage, what else—bereft of parents, ignoramuses—what do they say in your language—[114] (*Nobody thought that he would suddenly slump down into the jaws of death.*)

INGE (*in a gentle tone*). Bruno!

(*Silence. Nobody says a word, lest weeping breaks out. At this time, as a rain of bullets begins, all breathe a sigh of relief. Everyone rushes to stand at the barricade and start raining bullets—and Willi holds up a torn, burnt, red banner. Wallstrasse keeps fighting with life at stake, and in the dawn breeze the war-worn red banner flies as testament to their vow.*)

'Awake, awake, you who have lost all.'[115]

Curtain

---

114 In the video he inserts 'in your *polite* language' and repeats it before collapsing.

115 The Bengali translation of the leftist anthem *The Internationale*, with which the play ends. Bishnupriya Dutt notes that they used to playback the Soviet version, in Russian.